An Introduction to Google for the Older Generation

by

P.R.M. Oliver
and
N. Kantaris

Bernard Babani (publishing) Ltd
The Grampians
Shepherds Bush Road
London W6 7NF
England

www.babanibooks.com

D1321960

Please Note

Although every care has been taken with the production of this book to ensure that any projects, designs, modifications and/or programs, etc., contained herewith, operate in a correct and safe manner and also that any components specified are normally available in Great Britain, the Publishers and Author(s) do not accept responsibility in any way for the failure (including fault in design) of any project, design, modification or program to work correctly or to cause damage to any equipment that it may be connected to or used in conjunction with, or in respect of any other damage or injury that may be so caused, nor do the Publishers accept responsibility in any way for the failure to obtain specified components.

Notice is also given that if equipment that is still under warranty is modified in any way or used or connected with home-built equipment then that warranty may be void.

© 2010 BERNARD BABANI (publishing) LTD

First Published - February 2010

British Library Cataloguing in Publication Data:

A catalogue record for this book is available from the British Library

ISBN 978 0 85934 714 3

Cover Design by Gregor Arthur

Printed and bound in Great Britain for
Bernard Babani (publishing) Ltd

About this Book

To 'google' is now an accepted English verb. But Google is more than just an Internet search tool. *An Introduction to Google for the Older Generation* has been written to both help you use Google Search more effectively, and to explore some other tools offered by Google. Chapters include:

- Using **Web Search**, organising your life with the **Google Calendar** and your correspondence with **Google Mail**.

- Using **Google News** to easily keep abreast of World and local news as and when it happens.

- Using **Google Finance** to get instant up-to-date and historical data on stocks and shares, mutual funds, foreign currencies and public companies.

- Organising, editing and sharing your digital photos with **Picasa**, and your videos with **YouTube**.

- Using **Google Maps** to view maps and local business information, get driving, public transport and traffic information, view satellite imagery and walk through Street View imagery of some parts of the World.

- 'Flying' with **Google Earth** to anywhere on the globe and viewing satellite imagery, maps, terrain and Street View.

This book is produced in full colour and is presented using everyday language and avoiding technical jargon as much as possible. It was written with the Older Generation in mind who may have little knowledge or experience of using a computer. It will, of course, also apply to all other age groups. Google frequently makes changes to its programs, so if something we show is not quite the same, that is probably why. Have fun and enjoy your computing!

About the Authors

Phil Oliver graduated in Mining Engineering at Camborne School of Mines and has specialised in most aspects of surface mining technology, with a particular emphasis on computer related techniques. He has worked in Guyana, Canada, several Middle Eastern and Central Asian countries, South Africa and the United Kingdom, on such diverse projects as: the planning and management of bauxite, iron, gold and coal mines; rock excavation contracting in the UK; international mining equipment sales and international mine consulting. He later took up a lecturing position at Camborne School of Mines (part of Exeter University) in Surface Mining and Management. He has now retired, to spend more time writing and 'messing about in boats'.

Noel Kantaris graduated in Electrical Engineering at Bristol University and after spending three years in the Electronics Industry in London, took up a Tutorship in Physics at the University of Queensland. Research interests in Ionospheric Physics, led to the degrees of M.E. in Electronics and Ph.D. in Physics. On return to the UK, he took up a Post-Doctoral Research Fellowship in Radio Physics at the University of Leicester, and then a lecturing position in Engineering at the Camborne School of Mines, Cornwall, (part of Exeter University), where he was also the CSM Computing Manager. At present he is IT Director of FFC Ltd.

Trademarks

Android, **Chrome**, **Google**, **Gmail**, **PageRank**, **Picasa** and **YouTube** are registered trademarks of Google Inc.

All other brand and product names used in the book are recognised as trademarks, or registered trademarks, of their respective companies.

Contents

1

Searching with Google

Google, arguably the most popular search engine on the Internet, is a tool for finding resources on the World Wide Web. At some time, everyone that uses the Internet probably uses simple Google searches to find what they are looking for. We have been using them since Google first 'went public' in the late 1990s.

But Google is much more than just a search tool. Google is about organising the world's knowledge. It maintains indexes of Web pages and other online content such as photos, movies, books, business information, news, maps, scholarly papers, videos and music, and makes this information freely available to anyone with an Internet connection.

To pay for all this, Google generates its income with unobtrusive online advertising on its search results pages.

A Google Search Query

The life span of a Google search query normally lasts less than half a second, yet involves a number of different steps that must be completed before you get the search results on your screen, as shown in Fig. 1.1.

- The query is checked to match any advanced syntax and if it is spelled incorrectly a more popular or correct spelling variation is flagged.

- A check is made to see if the query is relevant to Google's vertical search databases (such as News, Books, Blogs, Images and Videos), and relevant links are chosen to go with the regular search results.

- In the Index Servers a list of relevant pages for the organic search result is prepared and ranked on page content, usage and link data.

- A list of relevant adverts is chosen for placement near the search results.

- The query then travels to Google's Doc Servers, which actually retrieve the stored documents and generate short 'snippets' describing each search result.

- Finally the search results are returned to you in a fraction of a second.

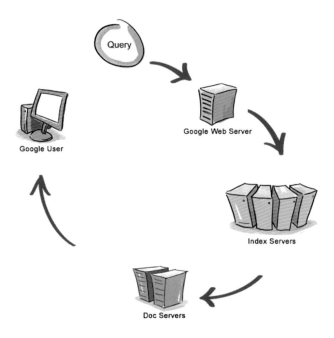

Fig. 1.1 The Life of a Google Search Query

Web Searches

As you all know, doing a search on Google is easy, but with a little more knowledge, you can get much more from Google. For a basic search in the UK, open the Google UK home page by typing **www.google.co.uk** into your browser's Address Bar, as shown below.

Fig. 1.2 Google Search Home Page for the UK

Then simply type the word, or phrase, that best describes the information you want to find into the **Search Box** and either, accept a drop-down AutoSuggest option, press the **Enter** key, or click the **Google Search** button.

Most Web browsers have an **Instant Search** box that lets you search the Web directly from the Address bar, as shown in Fig. 1.2 above. You just type your search query into this box. You may have to set Google as the tool to use (Fig. 1.2).

Google produces a results page, like the one shown in Fig. 1.3 on the next page, with a list of Web pages related to your search terms. It ranks the list with what it considers the most relevant match found at the top. Clicking any underlined link in the results list will take you to the related Web page.

Fig. 1.3 A Google Search Results Page

Note that in our example, Google recognised our spelling mistake, and searched for *pensions*, not *pensons*.

The Search Results Page

The results page contains lots of information about the search. Here we show and describe the parts of the page, starting from the top, and working from left to right.

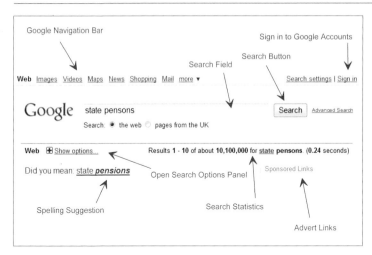

Fig. 1.4 Components of a Google Search Results Page

Google Navigation Bar – Click the link for the Google service you want to use. You can search the Web, browse for images, videos, maps, news, shopping, navigate to Gmail or click on **More** to access other Google tools.

Sign in to Google Accounts – Sign in to, or open, your Google Account. This lets you customise pages, view recommendations, and get more relevant search results.

Search Field – The text box where you type your search terms to start a Google search.

Search Button – Click this button to send a search query. This is the same as pressing the **Enter** key.

Search Options – These let you filter Web results by type, (videos, forums, and reviews) or according to when they were created or last updated, or filter Image results by size, type and colour.

Advanced Search – This links to a page on which you can do more precise searches.

Search Statistics – This describes your search, indicating the total number of results, and how long the search took to complete (0.24 seconds in our example).

Spelling Suggestion – If Google thinks you made a mistake entering your query, it will suggest another search term, depending on where you are located. It is quite intuitive and recognises that different terms and spelling are used in different parts of the world.

Image results for **swimming** - Report images

British **Swimming** & The ASA : Homepage
9 Oct 2009 ... British **Swimming** and the Amateur **Swimming** Association in the UK.
www.britishswimming.org/ - Cached - Similar

Book results for **swimming**
Open Water Swimming: A Complete Guide for ... - by Penny Lee Dean - 234 pages
Master the Art of Swimming: Raising Your ... - by Steven Shaw - 186 pages

Video results for **swimming**

 Mr. Bean goes to the swimming pool
4 min 13 sec.
www.youtube.com

 Efficient Swimming
2 min 58 sec
www.youtube.com

Fig. 1.5 Search Results with Different Content Types

Google's search results are integrated and can be made up of multiple content types, such as images, news, books, maps and videos. It searches across all of these content sources, integrates and then ranks the results for the best answers. Fig. 1.5 above shows image results, a Web page, some Book results, and YouTube videos from a set of results.

Page Title – The first line of any search result item is the title of the Web page found. If there is a URL instead then the Web page has no title.

Text below the Title – This is an excerpt from the results page with the query terms boldened.

URL of Result – This gives the Web address of the result.

Cached – Clicking this link will show you the contents of the Web page when it was last indexed.

Similar Pages – When you click this link, Google will search for other pages that are related to this result.

About Search Terms

With Google, choosing the right search terms is the key to finding the information you need. It is often better to use multiple search terms. If you're planning a vacation in Cornwall, you may do better searching for **vacation cornwall** than with the words by themselves. And if you are interested in fishing, then **vacation cornwall fishing** may produce even better results. Choose your search terms carefully as Google can only look for what you choose.

Google searches are **NOT** case sensitive. All letters, regardless of how you type them, will be understood as lower case, so there is no point using capitals.

By default, Google only returns pages that include all of your search terms, and the order in which the terms are typed will affect the search results. To restrict a search further, just include more terms.

Google ignores common words and characters such as "in" and "how", and single digits and letters, because they slow down a search without improving the results. If a common word is essential to getting the results you want, you can include it by putting a "+" sign in front of it, but make sure there is a space before the "+".

Another method for doing this is conducting a phrase search and putting quotation marks "" around two or more words. Common words in a phrase search, such as "where are you" are included in the search. Phrase searches are also effective when searching for specific phrases such as in names, song lyrics or poems.

I'm Feeling Lucky

You can force Google to go straight to what it considers the most relevant Web site for your query. To do this, enter your search terms on the Google home page as usual, but click the **I'm Feeling Lucky** button, instead of the **Google Search** button, as shown in Fig. 1.2. We must admit that we don't use this feature very often.

Special Search Features

In addition to providing easy access to billions of Web pages, Google Web Search has some special features that many people don't seem to know about. With these, the feature result appears at the top of the list of Web page results.

Some of these only apply to the USA, but some of our most popular and useful ones here in the UK are listed below. Please bear in mind though, that Google is always in a state of flux. New features are added quite often and by the time you read this, there may be many more of them, or some might have disappeared!

Try typing **www.google.co.uk/thingstodo** into the Address Bar of your browser (as described on page 3). It should produce a very colourful list of 50 suggestions, as shown below.

Fig. 1.6 Some 'Things to do' with Google

Weather

To see the weather for most UK towns and cities, type **weather** followed by the town name into a Google Search box and click the **Search** button. Sometimes a county or postcode is needed as well.

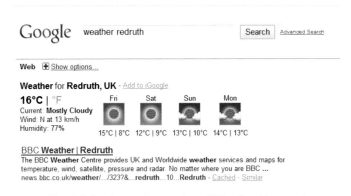

Fig. 1.7 Getting an Instant Local Weather Forecast

Time

To get the current time in most cities of the world, type in **time** and the name of the city, as we did for Sydney in Fig. 1.8 below.

Fig. 1.8 An Instant World Time Clock

If you type just **time** you will get the current time for wherever you are.

Cinema

If you want to go to the cinema, Google is the first place to look. Just type **cinema** followed by the name of your town into the Google search box, and click the **Search** button. You should get a result like ours in Fig. 1.9, listing the cinemas in the town showing details of the films being shown. Clicking the **Cinema listings for...** link will give you details of starting times, etc.

Fig. 1.9 Finding your Local Movies

To find details near you for a currently playing film, simply search for the film's name and enter the location details in the Search box, as shown in Fig. 1.10 below.

Fig. 1.10 Searching for a Particular Film

Search results for a film include a star rating (out of 5), snippets from online reviews, as well as links to the reviews themselves, and to trailers for the film. More than enough information to plan your evening!

Airline Travel Information

Fig. 1.11 Finding Current Flight Information

To check the flight status for domestic or international flights just type the flight number (such as sz103) into the search box, as shown above, and click on **Search**. This can be very useful if you have to meet an incoming flight. If you click the **Track status...** link you can track the full details of the flight in real time on the FlightStats Web site.

Google Q&A

Sometimes entering a simple question into Google, such as '**height of mount everest**' or '**when was tony blair born**' will come up with the answer at the top of the results page. With the former this was:

Elevation: 8,848 metres (29,029 ft)

Currency Conversion

Google has a built-in currency converter, so if you are going to Greece on vacation and want to take 1200 Euros with you, simply enter the conversion **1200 euros in pounds** into the search box and click on **Search**. The last time we did this the answer on the results page was:

 1200 Euros = 1 100.0307 British pounds

Fig. 1.12 A Currency Conversion Result

You don't get much for your pounds these days! If you don't know the currency of your target, just enter a simple search into the Google search box, like **turkey currency**, and then use the result (Turkish lira) for the conversion.

Local Business Searches

If you're looking for a store, restaurant, or other local business or service you can search for the category of business and the location and Google will return your information on the results page, with a map and contact information, as shown below for our search **bakers redruth**. Sometimes you have to add the county as well as the town, to get this to work.

Fig. 1.13 Results of a Typical Local Business Search

Spell Checker

Google checks whether any query you enter uses the most common spelling of a given word. If it thinks you're likely to generate better results with an alternative (or more correct) spelling, it will ask **Did you mean:**, Clicking the underlined suggestion starts a Google search for that term.

Maps

If you need a quick map to find a location or post code, just type in the name of the location, or post code, followed by '**map**' and Google will return a small map of the location.

Fig. 1.14 Generating a Quick Map

Clicking on the map will take you to a much more detailed version in Google Maps, which is described in Chapter 7.

Sports Results

Fig. 1.15 Finding Rapid Sports Results

To see scores and schedules for sports teams type the team name or league name into the search box. If you are lucky this will work for your team. Try entering **cricket** in the Google Search box and press **Enter**.

Dictionary

To get a quick definition for a word or phrase, simply type the word **define** followed by the word or phrase you want to know about.

Fig. 1.16 Using Google Search as a Dictionary

Calculator

Google Web Search includes another special feature which we think deserves a small section of its own, the calculator. This does not have a front-end, you just type your maths problem straight into the search box and get instant answers. As long as you have your browser open to the Internet it is always just a click away. The calculator will even recognise words as well as numbers.

The entries **nine plus six minus five**, or **9 plus 6 minus 5**, or **9+6-5**, all give the answer of 10.

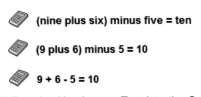

Fig. 1.17 Entering Numbers or Text into the Calculator

This very powerful feature lets you perform simple as well complex calculations using Google's search box. It can solve problems involving basic arithmetic, units of measure, conversions, and physical constants.

As well as text you can use the usual operators, **+** for addition, **−** for subtraction, ***** for multiplication, **/** for division, and **^** for exponentiation, or raising to the power of. In Fig. 1.18 we show how trigonometric functions can very easily be used.

Fig. 1.18 Using Trigonometric Functions in the Calculator

Making Conversions

One of the things that makes the Google calculator so useful for us is its ability to make conversions between types of units. As long as you label them, you can use mixed units in a query and even get your results converted to something else.

The terminology for conversions is:

(old units) in (new units)

The example in Fig. 1.19 below shows the use of automatic and forced conversions in the calculator.

Fig. 1.19 A Calculation Using Mixed Units

This is really an excellent feature and we strongly recommend you experiment with it.

Searching for Pictures

To use Google to search for images, such as photographs, icons, drawings and maps on the Web you can use an **Images** search. This gives you access to millions of indexed pictures which are available for viewing.

To do this, select **Images** on the Google Navigation Bar as pointed to in Fig. 1.20 below, type your query in the **Search** box, and click on the **Search Images** button.

Fig. 1.20 Starting an Image Search

Here we are searching the Web again for a local attraction, but this time we want pictures of it.

The results page, shown in Fig. 1.22 on the next page, opens with an impressive array of image thumbnails. You can select the size, or type, of images to be searched for by selecting from the **Show options** drop-down menu (Fig. 1.21).

Clicking on one of the thumbnails opens another page, see Fig. 1.23, with a frame at the top showing the image and giving some background on it, with the Web page on which the image is located open below.

Fig. 1.21 The **Show options** Menu

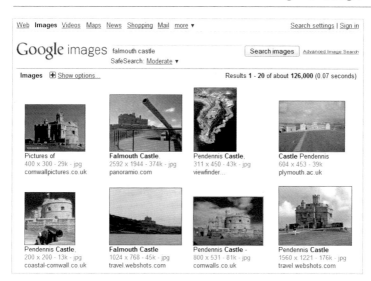

Fig. 1.22 Part of a Google Images Search Results Page

Fig. 1.23 Details of a Selected Image

In its search indexes Google analyses the text on the pages next to images, the captions and filenames of embedded images and other factors to make its image content selection for a search. The highest quality images are usually presented first in the results.

Fig. 1.24 The
SafeSearch Menu

If the Images results page contains photographs 'with adult content' and that is not what you wanted, you can click the **SafeSearch: Moderate** link to open the drop-down menu shown in Fig. 1.24, and select the **Strict** option.

As shown here, you can choose from three SafeSearch settings:

Off
No filtering. This turns off SafeSearch filtering completely.

Moderate
Most explicit images are filtered out from an Images Search, but ordinary Web search results are not filtered. This is the default SafeSearch setting, which will be active until changed.

Strict
This applies SafeSearch filtering to all your search results (both images search and ordinary Web search).

The default setting works well with us, but with some searches the **Strict** option may be needed. It's sometimes interesting to click between the three options to see how Google image 'censoring' works. At the end of the day, of course, the choice is yours.

No filtering can ever be perfectly accurate. If you have SafeSearch activated and still find sites containing offensive content in your results, you can click the **Report Offensive Images** menu option (Fig. 1.24). You can then tick the images you object to and hopefully Google will remove them from future results.

Have fun looking through the enormous volume of images available, but don't forget to come back and finish this book!

2

Google Calendar and Mail

If you are like us and have trouble keeping an ordinary diary up to date, then perhaps you should try doing it online. Google Calendar is a free Web-based calendar (or diary) application that lets you keep track of all your important events and appointments online. It works in a Web browser (such as Google Chrome, Microsoft Internet Explorer or Firefox), in which both JavaScript and cookies have been enabled. Then no matter where you are, once you are online, you will have access to your diary.

To create a new calendar from scratch, or to import an existing one, you need to start Google in your browser and click on the **more, Calendar** links on the Google Navigation Bar pointed to in Fig. 2.1 below.

Fig. 2.1 Opening the Calendar in a Google Chrome Browser

This opens the 'Sign in' window, (Fig. 2.2 on the next page), in which you can sign in to your Google Account if you have one, or click the Create an account button if you don't.

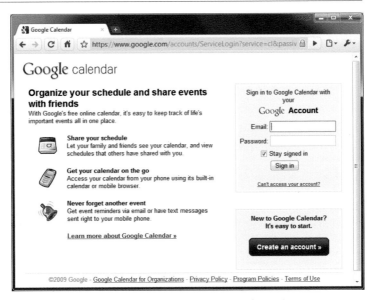

Fig. 2.2 Signing in to the Google Calendar

Creating a Google Account

You can't use Google Calendar (or Mail) unless you have an account with Google, so if you don't have an account click the **Create an account** button, fill out the required fields in the window that opens, and click **I accept. Create my account**. This procedure is necessary because the contents of your calendar will be kept online, or 'in the clouds' by Google. That way you can access them from anywhere by just signing in.

To check that the e-mail address you associated with your account is correct, Google sends a message to it. So check your e-mail for this verification message from Google. Open the message and click on the link provided to activate your Google Account. That's it done, you now have a Google account which you can also use for any of Google's online applications, such as GMail, Blogs, Reader, etc.

When you first sign in to Google Calendar a window similar to ours in Fig. 2.3 opens.

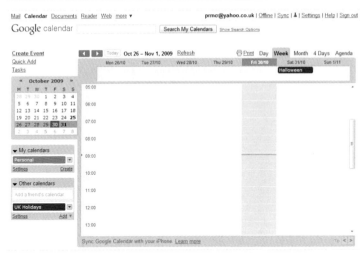

Fig. 2.3 A Newly Opened Google Calendar

Calendar Help

As you can see there is a lot on offer here, so perhaps the first thing to do is click the **Help** link on the top command bar which opens the quite detailed Help system, part of which is shown in Fig. 2.4 below. First try the **Getting Started Guide**

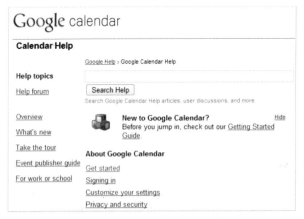

Fig. 2.4 Getting Help with Google Calendar

Calendar Views

There are five default ways to view your calendar which you control from the tabs on the bar above the work area.

Fig. 2.5 Controlling the Calendar Views

As shown, you can view just a day, a week, a month, 4 days, or the Agenda which is a text listing of your entries. To move through the calendar, click the **Back** ◀ or **Forward** ▶ buttons. The quick way to return to the current period (coloured yellow) is to click the Today button.

Adding Events

There are several ways to add entries (Events) to a Google calendar. The easiest is often to click the appropriate time slot in the working area to open a 'bubble box' like that in Fig. 2.6. You simply type in the details as shown here and click the **Create event** button.

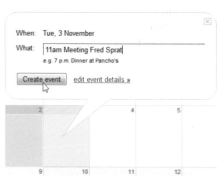

Fig. 2.6 Creating an Event

To add more to the Event click the **edit event details** link to open the screen shown in Fig. 2.7.

You might find it more convenient to start the procedure by clicking the **Create Event** link in the top left corner of the Calendar window, which opens straight to the screen of Fig. 2.7. Here you can enter or change the date, starting time, end time, location, and description of your event.

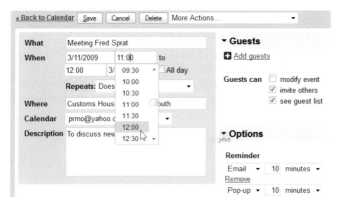

Fig. 2.7 Adding and Changing Detail to a Calendar Event

If you want to be reminded of the event, use the **Reminder** settings. You can choose to be reminded by e-mail, text message, or a pop-up message on your computer screen. When you are finished click the **Save** button, and admire the flag that appears. Added Meeting Fred Sprat on Tue 3 Nov 2009 at 11:00. Undo

Repeating Events

For repeating events such as birthdays, anniversaries or regular meetings, click the down-arrow in the **Repeats** box, select when you want the event repeated and then how often in the following entry box.

Fig. 2.8 Repeating Events

This is probably a good time to get out your family details and enter all the birthdays and anniversaries into your new calendar. If you set for e-mail reminders to be sent to you a few days before each one occurs you should never be caught short again. We certainly find any help like this to be indispensable these days!

Customising a Calendar

To customise your calendar, click the **Settings** link at the top right of the screen and in the General tab set your preferences for language, date format, default view, etc., as shown in Fig. 2.9 below. To apply your new preferences just click the **Save** button.

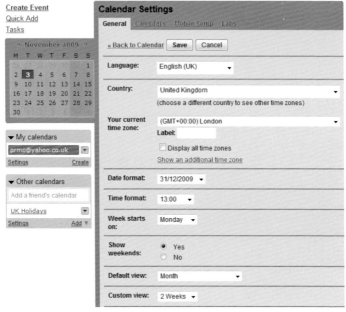

Fig. 2.9 Part of a Google Calendar Settings Sheet

Creating a Calendar

You can have multiple calendars with Google Calendar. This can be useful if you want to include other family members, or monitor a specific part of your life. We have separate calendars to keep track of some of our fixed rate financial bonds. To open a new calendar click the **Create** link in the **My Calendars** box, shown on the left in Fig. 2.9 above. Then give it a name and description and press **Create Calendar**.

Calendar Colours

Every calendar you create is given a different colour and its entries appear in that colour, as shown for our example in Fig. 2.10.

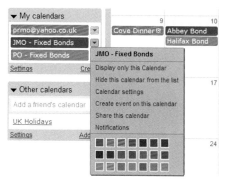

Fig. 2.10 Controlling Calendar Colours

To choose a different colour for one of the calendars, click the down-arrow against it and select a new colour from the options at the bottom of the displayed menu. This drop-down menu also gives you options to display and hide the calendar, change its settings, and you can even choose to share the calendar with other people.

When a calendar listed in the **My calendars** box is shown as a solid colour button all its entries will display in the main calendar working area (as in Fig. 2.10). If you have a lot of different calendars this can get somewhat confusing.

No problem though, when you don't want a particular one to show you can just click its entry in the **My calendars** box. This will 'switch it off' and temporarily remove its entries from the display. In Fig. 2.11 below we have done this for two of our calendars. Note how the calendar buttons have changed.

Fig. 2.11 Showing Two 'Switched Off' Calendars

Searching Calendars

As you might expect with Google you can search for items or events in either your own calendars or in other Public calendars. To do so, type a query in the text box at the top of the calendar screen and click the **Search My Calendars** button.

To see the type of queries you can use and where you can search, click the **Show Search Options** link next to the search buttons, to open the screen shown in Fig. 2.12 below.

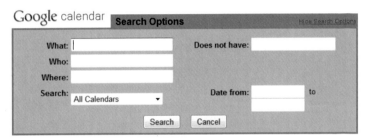

Fig. 2.12 Calendar Search Options

Google Mail

Google Mail, or Gmail for short, is a Web application that allows you to create, send and receive e-mail messages in your browser, and to store them freely and securely on Google's data sites. Your e-mail messages are then accessible to you at any time from anywhere. Gmail has some useful features:

- It lets you search your e-mail messages quickly and efficiently provided you archive rather than delete them.

- There is no need to delete messages as Google allows you around 7,000 MB of online storage space.

- It filters all your messages for spam so you don't have to worry on that score.

You can open Google Mail from any Google page by clicking the **Mail** link on the Google Navigation Bar (See Fig. 2.1). If necessary, 'Sign in' if you already have a Google account, or 'Sign up' if not, as described earlier in the Chapter. The first time we did this the following message screen displayed.

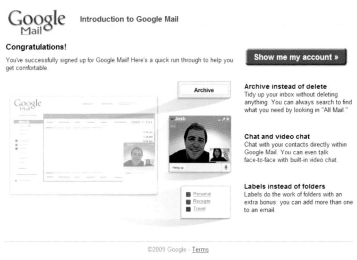

Fig. 2.13 Google Mail's Introductory Page

After reading the information on this page, clicking the **Show me my account** opens the **Inbox** of your Google Mail account page with some opening messages from the GMail Team, as shown in Fig. 2.14 on the next page.

You really should open each one of these by just clicking it. When you have finished in a message click the **Back to Inbox** link at the top and go to the next one.

Spend a while reading what they have to say and follow the links in each to **Customize Google Mail**, **Import contacts and mail**, and **Access Google Mail on your phone**. You should then be well set up for using Gmail.

If, like us, you are not interested in 'chatting' on your computer you can click on **turn off chat** in the **Google Mail view** section at the bottom of the mail window.

Fig. 2.14 The Google Mail Window

The Gmail Window

Apart from being Web based, the main difference between Google Mail and other e-mail programs like Windows Live Mail and Outlook, is that it automatically groups all your

e-mails with their answers into 'Conversations' so you don't have to organise your e-mails into different folders.

Thus, provided you don't delete any e-mails (but archive them instead), it is easy to find any e-mail you sent and it is then displayed together with all the answers you received on the subject. What a fantastic concept! Also, a single conversation can have several labels, so if a conversation covers more than one topic, you can retrieve it with any of the labels that you have applied to it.

Fig. 2.15
Options Menu

The other program options (Fig. 2.15) available on the left of the Gmail window, include:

Compose Mail – Opens a new message form for you to type a new e-mail.

Inbox – Returns a list of received e-mail messages. The number in brackets shows the number of unread messages.

Starred – Displays a list of your starred e-mail messages. To star a message, click the light blue star beside any message or conversation to give it a special status.

Sent Mail – Displays a list of messages you have sent.

Drafts – Displays a list of messages you have not sent.

6 more – Opens more options, including:

> **Chats** – Displays a history of your chats. Gmail's chat features allow you to make free voice calls by connecting you to the **Google Talk** network.

> **All Mail** – Displays all the messages you have received, sent, or archived, but not those you have deleted.

> **Spam** – Displays all e-mail messages that have been marked as spam.

> **Trash** – Displays all the e-mail messages you have deleted. Having looked at these, you can left-click the **Delete forever** option to remove deleted messages permanently. Messages left in the **Bin** for more than 30 days are deleted automatically.

Contacts

The Google Mail **Contacts** list allows you to store addresses, phone numbers, e-mail addresses and notes for all your contacts. Whenever you send an e-mail to someone, their e-mail address is added to your **Contacts** list automatically. By clicking on a contact you can view more information and all your conversations with that person. You can add a new contact manually by left-clicking the **Add Contact** link in the bottom-left of the window.

Composing a New Message

To compose and send a new message, click the **Compose Mail** link. This opens the window shown in Fig. 2.16.

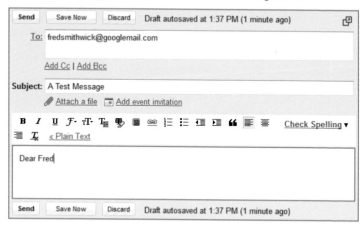

Fig. 2.16 Composing a New Message

In the **To:** box you type the recipient's e-mail address. If the person is in your **Contacts** list, then typing the first letter of a name will list all addresses starting with that letter. All you have to do is choose the appropriate one.

The best way to test out any unfamiliar e-mail features is to send a test message to your own e-mail address. This saves wasting somebody else's time, and the message can be very quickly checked to see the results.

Next, type a title for the message in the **Subject:** box. The text in this subject field will form a header for the message when it is received, so it helps to show in a few words what the message is about.

Finally, type your message and click the **Send** button.

Message Formatting

Gmail provides quite sophisticated formatting options for an e-mail editor. All the formatting features are self-explanatory.

If you hover the mouse pointer over an icon on the Format Bar, a bubble message opens telling you of its function, while left-clicking one either actions the formatting or displays options to choose from.

You should be able to prepare some very easily readable e-mail messages with these features.

Using E-mail Attachments

If you want to include an attachment with your main e-mail message, you simply click the ✐**Attach a file** link, under the **Subject** box, which opens a separate window displaying your Desktop, from which you can navigate to the file you want to attach. This could be a document, a photo, or indeed a video.

When you receive a message with an attachment, it displays with a paper clip to the right, as shown in Fig. 2.17 below.

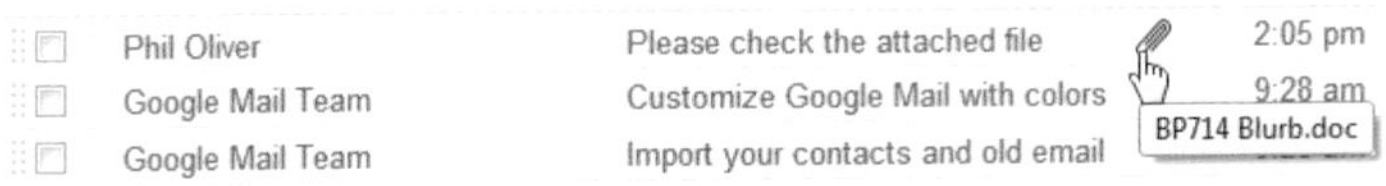

☐	Phil Oliver	Please check the attached file	✐ 2:05 pm
☐	Google Mail Team	Customize Google Mail with colors	9:28 am
☐	Google Mail Team	Import your contacts and old email	BP714 Blurb.doc

Fig. 2.17 A Received Message with an Attached File

Hovering the mouse pointer on the paper clip displays the name and type of the attachment. In our example the attachment contains a Word **.doc** file.

Right-clicking the attachment displays a choice of options, the main one being to save the attachment on your hard disc.

Left-clicking the e-mail or the attachment, opens the actual e-mail message with the attached file(s) below the text of the message. Clicking the attachment icon (in our case a Word document icon 📄) will open the file in its usual application. But you are given the option to abort this procedure if that's not what you really want to do.

Archiving E-mail Messages

To keep your **Inbox** tidy, messages that have been allocated suitable labels, by clicking the **Labels** button, can be archived. To do this, click the check boxes ☑ to the left of each message to select it, then simply click the **Archive** button.

If someone responds to a message that has been archived, the message and its corresponding conversations will reappear in your **Inbox**.

Archived messages can be found in the **All Mail** list by selecting an appropriate label, or searching for them.

*   *   *

Both Google Calendar and Google Mail have many more features which we are sure you will be able to explore for yourself. Good luck!

*   *   *

3

Google News

These days every newspaper and other news source has a Web site showing a continuously updated online version of its news and story contents. We all like to know what is happening and where, and if you are like us, some of these sites may be the first ones you visit whenever you switch your computer on.

Google goes one step further, it 'crawls' these news sites continuously, indexes their contents and presents a summary of the news as it happens in over 70 regional editions of Google News, including News UK shown below.

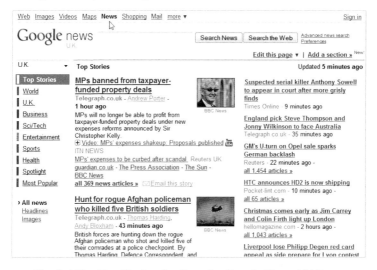

Fig. 3.1 The Top Stories Section of a Google News UK Page

To access Google News just click on the **News** link at the top of a Google page, or visit **http://news.google.com**.

To change between the different international versions of News use the drop-down menu in the top-left of the window, (showing **UK** in Fig. 3.1).

Google News Layout

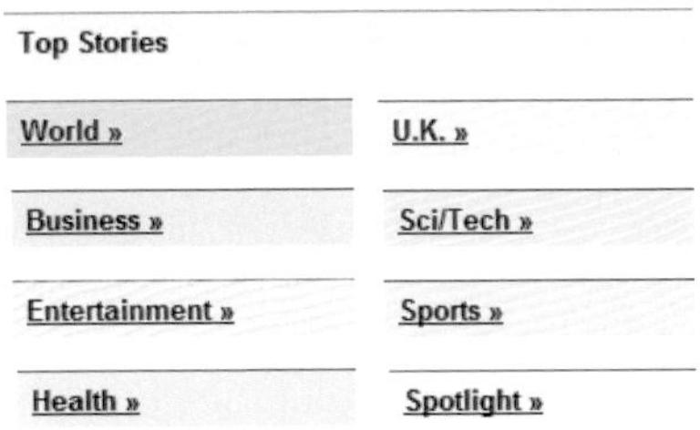

Top Stories	
World »	U.K. »
Business »	Sci/Tech »
Entertainment »	Sports »
Health »	Spotlight »

Fig. 3.2 Standard Google News Page Layout

The standard, or default, Google News page consists of the Top Stories section and eight standard sections, as shown in Fig. 3.2.

These are: World, Nation (UK in our case), Business, Sci/Tech, Entertainment, Sport, Health and Spotlight. These sections are available in all regional editions of Google News and are customisable.

The Top Stories section shows the most active stories throughout all sites, while the Spotlight section shows the most popular stories in the Google News edition actually being viewed.

About Google News

Google News is 'untouched by human hands' as the stories, headlines and photos you see on it are selected entirely by computer algorithms, based on factors like how often and where a story appears online. The grouping and ranking of stories depends on such things as titles, text, and publication time.

The standard Google News pages include news items published in the last 30 days, but Google doesn't throw the indexed data away then. It is included in the Google News Archive looked at later in the chapter.

News Clusters

Google groups News articles about the same story together, as shown here, and calls these groups, clusters. This makes it easy to read versions of the same news from different sources, or see how a story evolves over time. Clicking on

U.K. »

Mann 'very grateful' for pardon
BBC News - **1 hour ago**
Former British soldier Simon Mann, who was
jailed in Equatorial Guinea for his part in a coup
plot, is expected to arrive back in the UK on
Wednesday.
Telegraph.co.uk
⊞ Video: Simon Mann says he's grateful to have been pardoned
▶ ITN NEWS
British coup-plotter leaves Equatorial Guinea The Associated
Press
Sky News - Times Online - Telegraph.co.uk - guardian.co.uk
all 855 news articles » ✉ Email this story

Fig. 3.3 A Typical News Cluster

the link to see **all 855 news articles** (in our example) about a story will open a listing of the whole cluster.

How fresh a news story is, is shown by how long ago it was posted, e.g., **1 hour ago** for the one in Fig. 3.3 above. You click on the title to display the article, or one of the other links below.

Viewing Versions

Google gives you three ways to view its News. The default **All news** version with a few relevant photographs and some initial text detail (Fig. 3.1), a **Headlines** version with less detail and no photographs, or an **Images** version that lets you view and explore the top stories of the day through photos instead of just text.

> **All news**
> Headlines
> Images

You can easily switch between these views by clicking the links shown here, located at the top-left of a News page.

Fig. 3.4 on the next page shows an Images search. If you hover the mouse pointer over an image a box opens below with text details about the news item. You can click links in this floating box to go to the news story. Clicking a green **related images** link at the bottom of an image (pointed to in Fig. 3.4) opens images for all the stories listed. You can also search for image search results by entering a search string in the **Search Box**.

Fig. 3.4 Part of a Google News Page in Images Version

Which version you use is obviously up to you. Even if you prefer the more standard **All news** version with headlines, viewing News with Images can be very useful and often very enjoyable. Try an Images version search for your favourite sports team, model, celebrity or actress. The results can be pretty startling.

Searching Google News

You search Google News by entering your query and clicking on the **Search News** or **Search** button, depending on which page you are on.

Fig. 3.5 Searching Google News UK

By default, results are **Sorted by relevance** to your search terms as shown above. To see articles ordered chrono-logically you click on the **Sorted by date** link on the left of the results window (Fig. 3.5). You can also use the links on the left of the window to get news results from a particular period.

Where possible, Google adds videos to its news listings, as shown here. When there is a video available the ⊞ **Video** prefix is added to the article title. Just clicking this video link opens the YouTube video player directly on the page so you can watch the video, as in Fig. 3.6 on the next page. Clicking the link again closes the video. Maybe we can see now why Google bought YouTube a few years ago.

If necessary you can click the **Advanced news search** link on the News page, to confine your search to a specific news source, location, date range, or other criteria.

To limit a search to a specific country you can also specify a location for your search by entering your search terms into the search box followed by the controlling operator **location:country**. A search for **dolphins location:uk**, for example, would produce the latest news on dolphins in the UK. You can also specify a domain in the search box using the **site:** operator followed by a domain.

Biggest rise in car sales in 20 years
Telegraph.co.uk - David Millward -
1 hour ago
Car sales saw their biggest rise in 20 years with the motor industry recording a 31.6 per cent increase last month. By David Millward, Transport Editor A combination of the Government's "cash for bangers" scrappage scheme and a rush to beat next year's ...
Video: Car sales soar as scrappage scheme extended
ITN NEWS

0:07 / 0:59

Scrappage sees UK car sales surge BBC News
InTheNews.co.uk - Channel 4 News -
The Press Association - FT Alphaville (blog)
all 114 news articles » Email this story

Fig. 3.6 Running a YouTube Video on a News Page

If you are a soccer fan the search **football site:uk** gives all the latest news. In fact this type of news search term is good for using on personalised news pages as discussed next.

Searching News Archives

Google's News Archive Search gives an easy way to search and explore historical archives, such as major newspapers, magazines, news archives and legal archives. Remember that Google stores any news over 30 days old in its News Archives database.

You can search for events, people, things, or ideas and see how they have been described over time. Search results include content that is freely accessible to everyone and that which requires a fee to access. With the latter you can usually access an overview, or one viewing for free.

To use this feature, you can click the **Archives** link from the Google News home page, click the **Search Archives** button when there is one, or go to the News Archive Search page at:

http://news.google.com/archivesearch/

Fig. 3.7 Doing a News Archive Search for 'titanic'

An initial archives search will show articles from all dates ranked according to relevance, as shown in Fig. 3.7 above.

You can then click in the blue timeline bar graph, which shows graphically how the search results are grouped in time. Moving the pointer over a blue bar will show its date contents, and clicking one will give search results for that period and open another more detailed timeline for the selected period.

News for Mobiles

If you can access the Web on your mobile, you can access Google News with it as well, by just entering the address **m.google.com/news** into your phone's browser.

Fig. 3.8 Mobile News

Google News for mobile displays sources that are designed specifically for mobile Web browsers. You can access the day's top headlines, browse news in many categories, and find the story you are looking for on the go.

4

Google Finance

If you have a financial or business interest in company stocks and shares, mutual funds and international currency rates, then Google Finance will be for you. If not, you can probably skip this chapter. Google Finance offers an easy way to search for share prices, mutual fund details, and financial information on publicly listed companies. All the things pensions are made up from!

It has a clean, simple interface that is easy to navigate with relevant information right on the page in front of you. Historical price information is shown in very clever interactive graphs or charts, and it has links to a wealth of relevant additional information such as, recent news stories, comparable companies and company management details.

At the time of writing there were five versions of Google Finance, US, UK, Canada, Hong Kong and China. The UK version we look at here has been active since January 2008 so has had ample time to 'settle down'. It displays European company information, 20 minute delay actual and historical daily prices for LSE stocks back to 1996, other stock market and mutual fund data and GB£ currency quotes on its home page.

Accessing Google Finance

To open Google Finance UK, either click the **Finance** link from the **more** drop-down menu on the top of a Google UK page, as shown here, or go straight to the home page at **http://finance.google.co.uk**.

Finance UK Home Page

The opening page should look something like Fig. 4.1 below, but obviously with different content.

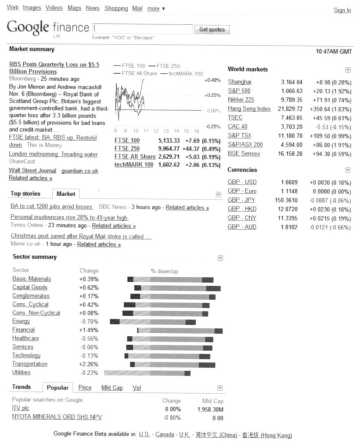

Fig. 4.1 Part of a Google Finance UK Home Page

The top section of the page (Fig. 4.1), consists of the usual Google menu along the top, with a **Get quotes** query entry box and button. You use this to search for prices of stock market companies, or mutual funds, using either their names or their ticker symbols.

Google have been very clever here with their Autosuggest feature.

As you type in the first part of a name a list instantly appears which

hl|		Get quotes
HL	Hargreaves Lansdown PLC	
HL	Hecla Mining Company	
ABNYY	ABN AMRO HLDG NV	
JARLF	JARDINE MATHESON HLD	
HLPPY	Hang Lung Properties Limited (ADR)	
HLDCY	Henderson Land Development (ADR)	

Fig. 4.2 Autosuggestion

suggests what you might be looking for. You just click the option you want in the list, the ticker symbol is automatically placed in the **Get quotes** box, and the home page changes to a detailed page of data on the security you searched for. This is very slick.

Market Summary

This gives an overview of the current UK financial situation, with access to the main news story on the left, summarises the main current FTSE indices, and shows the main currency exchange rates.

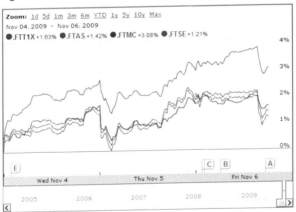

Fig. 4.3 FTSE Indices Chart

Clicking any of the index links in Fig. 4.1 gives you detailed current and historical data on it. Clicking the Market Chart above them opens an interactive chart comparing the performance of the four FTSE indices over time, as in Fig. 4.3. You can Zoom this chart, or drag the contents to see a different period.

News

News stories on Google Finance are presented by the Google News service seen in the previous chapter. The home page shows the **Top stories** for the **Market** generally, news for **Portfolio related** shares if you have a portfolio of shares open, or **Recent quote related** news if you don't. You click on tabs to move between these options.

Recent Quotes

The **Recent quotes** section displays current information about the stocks you have looked at recently. If you haven't looked at any, you will not see it! If you are signed in to Google any portfolios you have created will be shown here as well.

If you move the pointer over a stock's ticker symbol the full name will show in a message box, as shown in Fig. 4.4 for our favourite financial adviser. If you click the **Name** link its page of current detailed data will be opened.

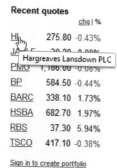

Fig. 4.4 Recent Quotes

Sector Summary

In the Sector Summary you can see at a glance how the major sectors are currently performing in the London financial markets. Scrolling over the bar charts will show you more detailed information about percentage increases and decreases for a given sector, as we show in Fig. 4.5.

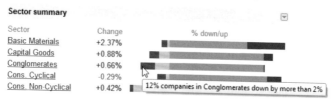

Fig. 4.5 Sector Summary Bar Charts

To get more detail on a sector, simply click its name to open its data page. This will show details of all the LSE companies in the sector, the top moving shares, related news articles and an interactive chart comparing the sector results with the FTSE 100 index.

Trends

Trends	Price	Mkt Cap	Vol		
Gainers				Change	
IMI plc				12.88%	
Inmarsat Plc				4.71%	
Prudential plc				4.58%	
Shire Plc.				3.74%	6,373.57M
Peter Hambro Mining plc				3.66%	2,181.31M
Losers				Change	Mkt Cap
Songbird Estates plc				-2.22%	1,442.95M
Rentokil Initial plc				-1.14%	1,883.79M
Dimension Data Holdings plc				-1.10%	1,223.97M
Lloyds Banking Group PLC				-0.67%	22,944.78M
Signet Jewelers Limited				-0.62%	27,373.95M

(menu shown: move to top / move up / move down / minimize)

Excludes stocks with mkt cap less than £1,000M. See FAQ

Fig. 4.6 The Trends Section

The **Trends** section allows you to see which companies are currently the biggest gainers and losers in terms of:

Price – % price change compared to the previous day.

Mkt Cap (Market Capitalisation) – change in market capitalisation, or the market value of the company, compared to the previous day.

Vol – lists the stocks with the highest traded volume.

To a certain extent you can customise the layout of the page using the ⊡ buttons on most of the sections. As shown in Fig. 4.6 above, clicking one of these opens a small menu which lets you **minimize** the section or move it up and down the page.

Company Searches

With Google Finance you can search for stocks, mutual funds or unit trusts, and public companies, using the **Get quotes** entry box described on page 42.

To see a list of the exchanges and indices covered by Google Finance you can click the **see disclaimer** link right at the bottom of the opening page. At the time of writing, quotations were real-time for the New York Stock Exchange and NASDAQ in the US and the Shanghai and Shenzhen exchanges in China, but the other International markets had time delays of between 10 and 20 minutes.

Fig. 4.7 on the facing page shows the results of such a search which gives an enormous amount of information. The 15 minute delayed share price is shown in the top left corner, with other trading and ratio details. Below is a chart correlating market data with corresponding dated news stories to help you determine if there was a relationship between them. You can also click and drag the chart to see different time periods and zoom out to see results for a longer period of time.

The **Related companies** shown are the ones Google considers to be similar in some way, so that you can make quick comparisons.

The **View all discussions** link offers quality Discussion groups with moderators to keep conversations "lively and spam-free".

The **Description** includes a précis history of the company and its aims. The **Officers and directors** section lists key personnel and sometimes even puts a face to a name. Sometimes when you place your cursor over an executive name, that person's details are displayed.

We think this is more than enough information to let you make informed judgements on whether to buy, sell or keep a company's shares.

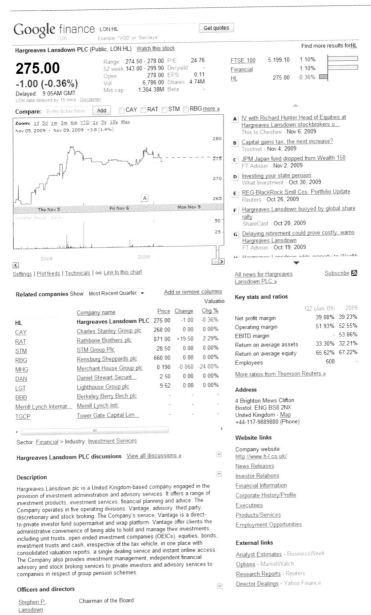

Fig. 4.7 Share Price and Company Information Page

Tracking Currencies

Google Finance offers data on how leading currencies are performing against each other. You can click a particular currency's link on the home page, such as GBP-USD, to go to a page with a history chart, relevant news, and current exchange rates for the main financial currencies.

Fig. 4.8 Currency Exchange Rates and Conversion

There is also a very useful currency converter at the bottom of the page, as shown in Fig. 4.8 above.

Your Own Portfolios

Google Finance lets you create and maintain portfolios of shares and mutual funds. This helps you to keep track of your investments and instantly know their actual value. It also gives you access to relevant financial information such as news and company management details. You can have as many portfolios in Google Finance as you like, with each holding up to 200 transactions.

To create a portfolio you need to be signed in to a Google Account (see page 20). Then you can click the **Portfolios** link on the left of the Google Finance page, as we did below.

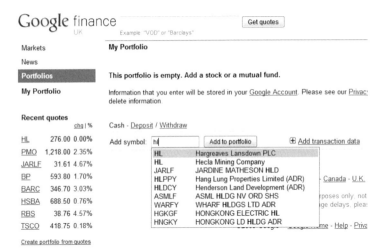

Fig. 4.9 Creating a First Portfolio

You use the **Add symbol** box to add a stock or fund and click the **Add to portfolio** button. From here you just plough straight in and add the transactions you want to show by clicking the **Add transaction data** link. If you want Google Finance to work out total values, etc., of your portfolio, each transaction needs details of at least the number of **Shares** and their **Price** (enter this in pence, not pounds). If you just want to watch a share, you can leave these blank.

Name	Symbol	Last price	Change	Shares	Cost basis	Mkt value	Gain	Gain %	Day's gain	Overall return
PRMO 1										Create a new portfolio »
Overview Fundamentals **Performance** Transactions										
Portfolios now support stock splits! Some of your pre-split transactions have been modified to remain correct when splits are considered. For details, see our Help Center.										
Compare Delete Import transactions I Edit transactions I Edit portfolio I Delete portfolio I Download to spreadsheet I Download to OFX										
Hargreaves Lansdown PLC	HL	276.00*	0.00 (0.00%)	500.00	1,000.00	1,380.00	+380.00	+38.00%	0.00	38.00%
Premier Oil PLC	PMO	1,222.00*	+32.00 (2.69%)	2,000.00	24,000.00	24,440.00	+440.00	+1.83%	+640.00	1.83%
BP plc	BP	593.50*	+9.60 (1.64%)							0.00%
Barclays PLC	BARC	347.05*	+10.55 (3.14%)							0.00%
Cash - Deposit / Withdraw										
Portfolio value:			+6.40 (2.54%)		£25,000.00	£25,820.00	+£820.00	+3.28%	+£640.00	3.28%

Fig. 4.10 A Portfolio with a Few Transactions Entered

In Fig. 4.10 we have added two stock holdings, and two we want to track. The portfolio is shown in **Performance** view but there are three other views you can use, all available on the text menu bar, these are: **Overview**, **Fundamentals**, and **Transactions**.

The **Edit portfolio** option lets you change the sorting of entries within a portfolio, or quickly add or delete portfolio entries, by adding or deleting their ticker names.

The **Edit transactions** option lets you add or edit data for specific transactions in the portfolio, such as **Date**, number of **Shares**, **Price** paid for a security, the **Commission** paid or **Notes**. To finalise any changes made, you have to click the **Save changes** button.

To delete a portfolio from your account click the **Delete Portfolio** link and then click the **OK** button to **Permanently delete this portfolio and all transactions in it**.

To add another portfolio to your account, click the **Create a new portfolio** link at the top-right of any of the portfolio pages, give the new portfolio a name, and click **OK**.

* * *

Good luck using Google Finance, we certainly enjoy it. But lets hope you have more 'luck' with your investments than we do!

5

Picasa for Your Photographs

Google has two main applications you can use for viewing and handling digital photographs. You can organise and edit your photos on your computer using **Picasa**, and store and display them online with **Picasa Web Albums**.

To work with videos, Google also has **YouTube**, the free service that allows anyone to view and share videos online.

About Picasa

 Picasa is a free downloadable program from Google that helps you find, edit and share all the pictures on your computer. Each time Picasa is opened, it automatically locates any new pictures and sorts them into 'folders'. It also has very powerful tools for editing your photos, almost making that expensive graphics program redundant. Picasa Web Albums lets you download and store your photos online, making them easy to share with the rest of the World. For a free program, it really has a lot to offer.

To use Picasa your computer needs to run under Windows 7, Vista, or XP and have at least 256MB of RAM and 100MB of available hard disc space. Most do these days.

At the time of writing Picasa 3.6 is the current version so that is the one we have used here. It really is a great program and deserves a book on its own.

To get Picasa, go to **http://picasa.google.com** which opens the screen shown in Fig. 5.1 on the next page. When you have viewed the video and read about Picasa 3.6's new features, press the **Download Picasa 3.6** button to start the process.

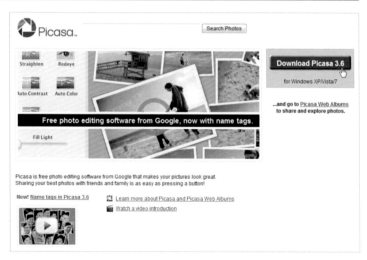

Fig. 5.1 The Picasa Home Page

If asked, opt to **Run** the download file, read the License Agreement and click **I Agree**, accept the destination folder suggested for the download (or **Browse** to another location), and click **Install.**

Once the program is installed, the box shown in Fig. 5.2 is opened. We suggest you select for a limited scan of your PC, as shown here, or you may be surprised at the results. You can always add more locations later. If you let Picasa scan your

Fig. 5.2 Giving Scan Instructions

entire computer, it will find cached Internet files, graphics from computer programs, and other images that you probably don't need in your photo album. You can remove files later, but it's much easier not to import them in the first place.

The Picasa Window

When Picasa opens for the first time it lists all of your photos by date retaining the same file structure as your hard drive, as shown for us in Fig. 5.3.

Fig. 5.3 Picasa's Opening View on our Computer

To understand Picasa it is important to remember that the program scans your computer for photos, and displays them for you. It does not keep, copy, or store, your photos, they are always maintained in their original files on your hard disc. But it does keep and process references to them which it stores in its own database. **If you delete a photo from a folder in Picasa, the photo will be deleted from the folder on your computer.** So beware.

On the left of the Picasa window (Fig. 5.3) is a Folders List pane, with the main working area, or library, to the right displaying thumbnails of the images in the selected folder. Although the thumbnails are grouped by the folders on your hard disc, you can continuously scroll through thumbnails of all of your photos, using the scroll bar on the extreme right or by rolling your mouse wheel. So in the working area you can access any photo on your computer without having to physically open its folder.

The scroll bar is a little unusual and needs some comment. If you are looking in the middle of a folder, clicking the ⌃ icon moves you to the top of the folder. Clicking it again moves you up to the top of the next folder. Clicking the ⌄ icon moves you down to the top of the next folder below. Clicking the ⌃ and ⌄ icons move you up or down one row of thumbnails. You can also drag the central slider to move the thumbnails up or down continuously. To move quickly through a large number of photos, locate the folder you want in the Folders List on the left and click it. All this sounds a little heavy, but it works well once you try it.

Although you can continuously scroll through your folders of thumbnails, you always know where you are in the list as a header bar is placed between the folders, like the one shown in Fig. 5.4 below.

Fig. 5.4 A Typical Picasa Folder Header Bar

The buttons on the Header bar allow you to carry out actions on the photos in the folder. We will look at these later on.

Changing Thumbnail Size

The easiest way to change the size of thumbnails in Picasa is to drag the Thumbnail Slider ⊏━━━◯━━━⊐ at the bottom of the working area. You can also use the **View**, **Small Thumbnails**, or **View**, **Normal Thumbnails** menu options, or the **Ctrl+1** and **Ctrl+2** keyboard shortcuts.

To look at the detail in your photos when browsing your library, click and drag the **Loupe** tool 🔍 next to the slider.

Fig. 5.5 Using the Loupe Tool

A round magnifying glass appears as shown in Fig. 5.5. As soon as you release the mouse button it will disappear.

You can also view a photo full size while working with thumbnails. Just select, or move the pointer over, a thumbnail and hold down the **Ctrl+Alt** keys together. Releasing the keys returns you to where you were.

Folders and Albums

As we have seen, the Folders List on the left of the Picasa window displays all your collections in Picasa. You may have noticed by now, though, that this does not just hold folders but 'Albums' and 'People' as well. As shown in Fig. 5.6, your collections will normally include:

Fig. 5.6

Albums   These are virtual folders that let you group related photos without moving your files around the disc. Albums only contain references to your picture files (which live in folders). They have green ☀ or ▦ blue icons. You can create a new album with the **New Album** button ⊕▦.

Folders   These contain files stored on your
                          hard drive that have been scanned.
                          They have a yellow 📁 folder icon.

People   To organise your photos by the
                          people in them Picasa uses facial
                          recognition technology to find and
                          group similar faces together across
                          your entire collection of photos.
                          Moving or deleting faces from a
                          People Album does not affect the
                          original files on your hard disc.

Projects   Picasa projects, like Movies, Collages,
                          and Screen Captures 📷, are stored in
                          a directory named Picasa on your
                          hard disc and appear as Projects in
                          the Folders List. If you have not
                          actually created any of these, this
                          folder will not show.

Exported Pictures These are folders of photos that you
                          have exported from Picasa. 📁

Hidden Folders   These are folders that you have
                          hidden, so that no one else can
                          access them. 📁

Other Stuff   This has Folders containing videos or
                          small image files (less than 250 x 250
                          pixels), or unusual image files. 📁

Folder Hierarchy

You can change the view of the Folders List with the **View**,
Folder View menu command, and selecting from the default
Flat Folder View, **Tree View**, or **Simplified Tree View**
options. The first two of these are also available with the
▤ ▤ toggle button at the top of the Folders List.

Flat Folder View is the default view and displays all the
'watched' and 'scan once' folders on your computer.

Tree View is a hierarchical view of all the 'watched' folders on your computer.

Simplified Tree View is a semi-hierarchical view of the folders which contain most of your photos, which may not actually reflect the folder structure of your disc.

Organising Your Photos

How you organise your photographs is obviously a personal choice. Some people just put them all into one folder and use Picasa to separate them into logical groupings or albums. We prefer to create a new dated folder (such as 2010_03_02) for every batch of photos we download from our camera, then it is easy to sort the folders in date order in Windows.

You can move thumbnails by simply dragging them from folder to folder in Picasa, and it will confirm and move the corresponding files on your hard drive. This makes it very easy to organise your photographs. If you want to drag an entire folder into another folder first select it with the **Ctrl+A** keyboard shortcut.

To permanently delete a photo from your computer using Picasa, just right-click it in a library folder and select **Delete from Disk** from the context menu. Clicking **Yes** in the **Confirm Delete** box will send it to the Windows recycle bin. If you delete a photo from an Album, it just removes it from the album. The photo itself remains in its folder.

If you drag a photo from one folder to another folder within Picasa, the photo changes actual folders on the disc. If, on the other hand, you drag a photo from a folder to an album, the album references the photo and appears to have the photo in it. But its file still physically sits in its folder.

To remove duplicate pictures from your Folders or Albums, right click the image and select **Hide**. The photo should be instantly removed from Picasa, but not deleted from your hard disc.

The Photo Tray

When a folder is first selected, all the photos in it are 'effectively' selected and a small thumbnail appears in the Photo Tray (at the bottom-left of

Fig. 5.7 The Photo Tray

the Picasa window) with the number of photos on it, as shown here in Fig. 5.7.

To select a single photo in the Picasa library, just click on it. To select multiple photos in the same folder, keep the **Ctrl** key depressed and

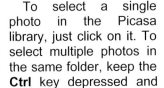

Fig. 5.8 The Photo Tray

click them. Their thumbnails will then appear in the Photo Tray, as shown in Fig. 5.8. It displays the photos you currently have selected.

When you want to select photos from multiple folders or albums, you have to click the **Hold** button  to anchor the thumbnails in the Photo Tray before moving to another folder. A green marker ⊙ is placed on held thumbnails. Clicking the **Clear** button ○ will remove selected photos from the Photo Tray. The **Add To** button ▮▾ lets you add the selection from the Photo Tray to an existing or a new Album.

Face Recognition

With Picasa 3.6 face-matching helps you organise your photos according to the people in them. The first time you open Picasa, it will scan your photos for new faces. It can take some time to scan all your photos ▦ Scanning, 51% complete , almost a day for us, and we were left with over 5,000 **Unnamed People** which needed manual recognition.

To add name tags, click on the Unnamed entry ▦ Unnamed (3,352) at the top of the **People** collection which shows all of the unrecognised faces in your photos collection.

Fig. 5.9 Adding a Name to a Group of Unnamed People

Each face thumbnail in this album represents a group of 'similar' faces that have been found. Adding a name to one face gives the same name to all the faces in the group. To see this, click the **People** button which opens the People tab on the right, as shown in Fig. 5.9.

Click in the **Add a name** box under a face and type a name. As you type, Picasa searches your contacts and previous entries and offers matches (as above). Either select a name or type a new one and press **Enter** to create a new individual album in the **People** list.

As you won't want to name all the faces offered, you can just click the ✖ icon to place unwanted ones in the **Ignored** album.

Fig. 5.10 A People List

If you see an orange question mark ❓ next to a people album, you need to confirm or reject the suggestions made. Just click to keep or to remove photos from the album.

Fig. 5.11 An Example of a People Folder

After a few hours and maybe a glass or two of wine you should end up with a very useful feature. Just clicking on any of the names in the **People** list will open thumbnails of all their pictures on your computer, as in Fig. 5.11 above.

Tags and Stars

You can also give your photos 'tags' or 'stars', and search for photos with these attributes when you want them. You could tag all the photos of a certain place, or with a favourite pet, for instance. You can add multi-word tags to your photos and they are stored in the actual photo files themselves.

The blue status bar below the Picasa library `Tags: Ship Inn, Porthlevan` shows any tags that have been applied to your picture. To add a tag, select one or more photos and click the **Tags** button `Tags` in the bottom-right of the Picasa window, or use the **Ctrl+T** keyboard shortcut. These open the **Tags** pane shown in Fig. 5.12 on the facing page.

Here you can either click on one of the **Quick Tags** listed at the bottom, or type a new tag in the **Type in a tag to add** box and click the **Add** button +.

To set what appears in the **Quick Tags** list click the **Configure Quick Tags** button ⚙ and add or delete tags in the dialogue box that opens. Then click the **OK** button.

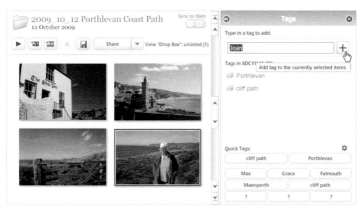

Fig. 5.12 Adding Tags to a Photograph

In Picasa you can mark special photos in your collections with 'stars'. They are then automatically added to the **Starred Photos** Album for you to process as you want. To do this, just select the photo and click the Star button. A small yellow star is placed on the thumbnail, as shown here. The **Star** button is a toggle button so to remove the star you just click it again.

Searching for Photos

It is no surprise that a program as powerful as Picasa has some very good searching facilities built in. These are found on the toolbar above the photo library as shown in Fig. 5.13.

Fig. 5.13 The Photo Filter and Search Options in Picasa

This shows both the search and filter tools and the green info bar that appears underneath when you use them. You can search for text associated with your photos, including filenames, tags, captions, Folder names, Album names, Collection names and camera maker. You just type your search term in the ⌕ ▭ Search Box.

As you type each letter, the search results instantly change, as shown in Fig. 5.14, and a new **Search results for...** Album is added to the top of the Folders List. To clear a search, press the **Esc** key, or click the red **Clear your search** button ❎ in the Search Box, or click the **Back to View All** button shown in Fig. 5.13.

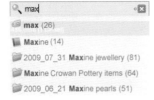

Fig. 5.14 Picasa Search Result List

You can filter your library photos by **date range** by moving the Slider shown in Fig. 5.13; to show only **starred photos** ★ , only **uploads to Web Albums** ↑ , only **photos with faces** 👤 , to show **movies only** ▦ , or to show photos with Geotags 📍 .

Editing and Fixing Photos

When you double-click on a photo in the library, Picasa opens it in an editing window where you can fix common problems and create great effects in your photos. As shown in Fig. 5.15 there are three editing tabs filled with tools to help you improve your photos.

Basic Fixes   Buttons that work in one to two clicks to remove **Redeye**, **Crop**, **Auto colour**, **Auto contrast**, **Straighten**, **Fill light**, **Retouch** and add **Text** to your photos. Try the **I'm Feeling Lucky** button, it might just sort your photo out automatically.

Tuning   More advanced editing features with sliders to help you fix contrast and remove colour cast. Select from **Fill Light**, **Highlights**,

Shadows, **Color Temperature**, and a **Neutral Color Picker**.

Effects   Effects are designed to help you turn a grey sky blue, brighten colours, and add photographic filters. There are 12 effects to choose from **Sharpen**, **Sepia**, **B&W**, **Warmify**, **Film Grain**, **Tint**, **Saturation**, **Soft Focus**, **Glow**, **Filtered B&W**, **Focal B&W**, and **Graduated Tint**.

Fig. 5.15 Editing a Zoomed-in Photo in Picasa

At any stage you can cancel your editing with the **Undo...** button. Details of any changes you make to a photo are saved in the Picasa database and a **.ini** file is also saved with the photo. The original photo file is not changed at all. As long as you use Picasa to handle your photos in the future this is fine. Otherwise use the **Save edited photos to disk** button (Fig. 5.3) or the **File**, **Save** menu command. Picasa then creates a copy of your photo with all your edits applied and moves the original to a hidden subfolder called 'picasaoriginals'.

Loading from Your Camera

With Picasa it is a doddle to transfer photos directly from your digital camera to your computer. If necessary, click Picasa's desktop icon to start the program, connect your camera to the computer (usually with a USB cable) and switch the camera to Computer or maybe Playback Mode. Clicking the import button [🖷▶ Import] will start the procedure and open the Import tab shown in Fig. 5.16 below.

Fig. 5.16 Importing Photos from a Digital Camera

Your camera should be recognised as ours was as the K:\ drive above. If not, click the **Import from:** button and select from the drop-down list.

In the **Import to:** boxes at the bottom you control where the imported photos will be placed. Choose the parent folder on your hard disc and type its new name in the **Folder title:** box. Note that Picasa offers you the current date as a folder name. We usually just add some descriptive text to this.

There are options to delete the original photos from your camera, but we prefer to do that manually and would recommend leaving the default **Leave card alone** option selected.

Then either click the **Import All** button , or select the photos you want to import and click the **Import Selected** button. In our case we have selected 14 photos out of the 50 on the camera. The new photos should be downloaded to your hard disc and appear straight away in Picasa. This is the easiest way we have found so far.

If at any time you don't think Picasa is scanning a folder and is not keeping its contents up to date in the library, use the **Tools**, **Folder Manager** menu command and check the settings in the Folder Manager shown in Fig. 5.17. Watched folders should have the **Scan Always** mark ⟳ next to them. The **Scan Once** ✔ option gets Picasa to scan the folder, but not to look in it for updates in the future, and the **Remove from Picasa** option ✖ stops Picasa checking a folder at all.

Fig. 5.17 Controlling the Folders Scanned by Picasa

Using Your Photos

Once you have mastered Picasa and have all your photos organised the way you want, there is a large list of things you can actually do with them. These are most easily accessed with the buttons on one of the following two toolbars.

Fig. 5.18 The Library Toolbar

The tools in the small toolbar above the Library pane (Fig. 5.18) act on all of the photos in the currently active Folder or Album.

Fig. 5.19 The Photo Tray Toolbar

To mix photos from different Folders and Albums, first place them in the Photo Tray and then use the tools in the bar to the right of the Photo Tray, shown in Fig. 5.19 above.

Playing a Slideshow

A slideshow is perhaps the first thing you'll want to do once you have your photos as and where you want them. Clicking the **Play Fullscreen Slideshow** button will start one for the photos in the current Folder or Album.

You can control the show, once it has started, with the settings on the bar shown in Fig. 5.20 which appears on the screen when you move the mouse pointer. Hopefully, these should all be fairly self explanatory.

Fig. 5.20 Controlling a Slideshow

Photo Collages

Picasa 3.6 has a collage maker with seven different collage themes to use, ranging from a simple **Contact Sheet**, as shown below, to a **Picture Pile** theme in which you can arrange, re-size and rotate your photos and choose the background.

Fig. 5.21 Creating a Photo Collage

You really must play with this tool; you can get some very good results. We especially like combining images from the People Folders into **Picture Pile** collages. You must also try the **Multiple Exposure** option, which superimposes all the pictures in the Album. This is best done with a small number of photos though!

When you get one you really like, just clicking the **Desktop Background** button will make your photo collage into the Windows desktop wallpaper. You can also print, e-mail or upload them.

Movie Presentation

 In Picasa 3.6 you can take a collection of photos and videos and combine them into a movie, complete with soundtrack. You can easily add your own title slides and then post your creation to the Web with one click. We will leave it to you to find your way here, we just do not have the space.

Printing Photos

 You can select a photo or a range of photos and print them from Picasa by clicking the **Print** button. This opens the box shown in Fig. 5.22.

Fig. 5.22 Printing Photos from Picasa

You have many print options here, but we prefer to set the **Print Layout** to **Full Page** and click the **Printer Setup** button to control the printing layout from the printer software.

 If you click the **Shop** button on the Photo Tray toolbar, you can order prints of your photos online from a range of different printing services.

Sharing Your Photos

With the **Share** button ⸤ Share ▾ ⸥, you can send the photos in the current Folder or Album to someone else. The photos are first uploaded to a Picasa Web Album.

You can select photos and click the **Email** button ⸤◌⸥ to send them as attachments with a message. Picasa opens your e-mail program to do this.

You can also post selected photos directly to your Blogger account by clicking the **BlogThis** button ⸤B⸥.

The **Export** button ⸤◌⸥ lets you save copies of your edited photos. You can change the image size and quality or add a watermark to the exported photo.

Finally you can use the **Upload** button ⸤↟⸥ to send the photos in the Photo Tray to a folder in your Picasa Web Albums space, provided by Google somewhere in the clouds.

The **Geotag** button ⸤◌⸥ gives you an easy way to embed location information within your photo files so that you can display them on Google Earth satellite maps for your friends to see. Longitude and latitude information is written to the photo's EXIF GPS metadata.

Picasa Web Albums

With Google, you organise and edit your photos on your computer using **Picasa**, and then you can store and display them online with **Picasa Web Albums**, which lets you upload and share your photos quickly and easily on the Web. Once you have registered, you get 1GB of free storage space for your photos, but if this is not enough, you can upgrade and pay for even more space.

The **Sync to Web** button ⸤◌◌⸥ in Picasa 3.6 lets you synchronise specific Folders or Albums on your computer to the Web. If you edit or add photos to these Folders or Albums on your computer, the changes will be automatically reflected in Picasa Web Albums online.

Uploading to Web Albums

To place your photos on the Web for all to see, open Picasa and select the photos that you want to 'publish'. To select multiple photos, press the **Ctrl** key while clicking the photos. Click the **Hold** button if you want to select from another Folder or Album. Your selected photos appear in the Photo Tray at the bottom-left of the Picasa window. When you have selected all the photos you want, click the **Upload to Web Albums** button 🔺. If you are not signed in to your Google Account, you should do this and, for the first time, provide information to set up your Web Album account. The **Upload to Web Albums** box then opens, as shown below.

Fig. 5.23 Uploading to Web Albums

Click the **New** button to create a new folder and fill in the **Album Title** and **Description** boxes. Make sure the **Public Album** radio button is selected, and click the **Upload** button. The Upload Manager will open and display the status of the upload. When the upload is complete, click the **View Online** button to launch the album in your browser.

You can open Web Albums at any time from Picasa by clicking the **Web Albums** link at the top of the window. If you don't want to work with Picasa, you can open it from the top of any Google page by clicking the **more, Photos** links. We will leave it to you to explore Web Albums further. We find it great fun, but don't let yourself become addicted!

Backing Up Your Photos

You can use your Web Albums space to back up your photos, but make sure you upload using the **Original size** option in the **Size to upload** drop-down list of the **Upload to Web Albums** box. This will use up your 1GB of space in about 300 average photos, so you may have to **Upgrade**.

Perhaps a better option, especially if you have an external hard disc, is to use Picasa's **Tools, Backup Pictures** menu command, click the **New Set** button and start a full backup of all your photos.

The Photo Viewer

When you install Picasa, the Picasa Photo Viewer is also installed, which lets you take a quick look at your images without having to use Picasa itself.

From your desktop or from within a Windows Explorer window, just double-clicking an image file will launch the Viewer, as shown in Fig. 5.24 on the next page.

The Viewer is usually opened with a full screen view but if you click outside the image boundary, the image will display in a window. If you double-click the image in the window it will display full screen again. Double-clicking again will zoom the photo. Rotating the scroll wheel on your mouse will step you through other photos in the same folder.

Fig. 5.24 The Picasa Photo Viewer Working in a Window

When you move the pointer to the bottom of the open image, a menu bar appears, as shown in Fig. 5.24. This shows a ribbon of thumbnails of the photos in the folder. Clicking one will jump the Viewer to that image. It also has buttons that let you zoom in and out, open Picasa to edit the photo, start a slideshow, upload the photo to Web Albums, rotate the image, add a star to it, and start other Picasa options.

At any time in Picasa, you can reconfigure the file types that the Photo Viewer will display with the **Tools, Configure Photo Viewer** menu command. We like this feature so much we have set it as our default viewer for all the photo types. If you don't feel the same just select the **Don't use Picasa Photo Viewer** option.

* * *

You can do a lot more with Picasa and Web Albums, but we leave it to you to find out how. We have set out here to get you up to speed with the basics, and the rest really should be no problem to you. We hope you get as much enjoyment from Picasa as we do though!

6

YouTube

 These days people seem to have an incredible desire to swap video clips with each other, and that's where **YouTube** comes in. It is a video sharing Web site, owned by Google, where anyone can view, upload, and share video clips. According to Google, people are watching hundreds of millions of videos a day on YouTube, so it's really a huge repository of video clips. YouTube is free as it is partially supported by advertising.

YouTube was first created in February 2005 but it caught on very quickly and only 18 months later Google purchased it for US$1.65 billion. By January 2009 over 100 million YouTube users had made over 5 billion video viewings.

YouTube has become so popular so quickly mainly because it is very easy to use. It accepts most common video formats and converts them so that they can be viewed over the Web without special software. So anybody can upload video clips from their digital cameras or mobile phones, and friends can view them without worrying about the format. You can also e-mail the link to friends easily, or add YouTube generated code to your Web page or blog so a video can be played from the page.

Finding Your Way Around

To start YouTube you can type **www.youtube.com** into the Address Bar of your browser and press the **Enter** key. Or you can open it from the top of any Google page by clicking the **more**, **YouTube** links. A page similar to ours in Fig. 6.1 should open.

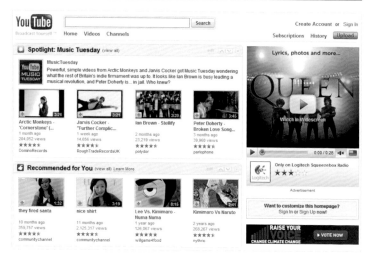

Fig. 6.1 A YouTube Opening Screen

The Home Tab

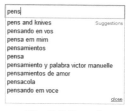

Fig. 6.2 Search
Suggestions

The YouTube opening screen as shown above, has a **Search** box at the top. You enter text here to search for the type of video content you want to watch. This **Search** box has Google's search-suggest feature built-in, so you get query suggestions as you type like the ones in Fig. 6.2. These apparently are based on the most popular search queries sent in to Google. They should save a few keystrokes, reduce spelling errors, and "improve the overall search experience".

The Home page has a small selection of ⬛ **Videos Being Watched Now**, and once you start using YouTube you get a ⬛ **Recommended for You** section. Below these are some ⬛ **Featured Videos** selected by YouTube editors, and of the ⬛ **Most Popular** videos. Clicking any of these will open the selected video for you to watch.

Each video listed has a title and image (you can click either to watch the video), a short description and some statistics, as shown in Fig. 6.3.

Fig. 6.3 The Layout of a Typical YouTube Listing

The Videos Tab

Clicking the **Videos** link on a YouTube page opens the **Videos** tab where you can more rapidly get a feel for YouTube. This has a list of video **Categories** (Fig. 6.4), and lets you rapidly look through some of the offered videos.

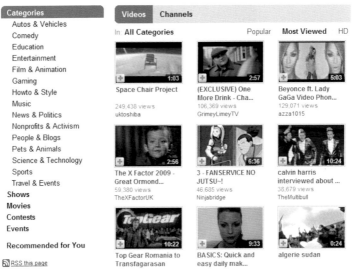

Fig. 6.4 The Videos Tab and Categories Menu

So far we haven't found much serious content you might be saying, but don't worry it is there on YouTube, you just have to dig a little deeper to find it.

The Channels Tab

In YouTube a **Channel** is a customised user's page, containing a user's profile information, videos, favorites and whatever else they want to share. YouTube is so popular now that its users are not only individuals publishing short clips, but large corporate bodies, the Queen, universities and public departments. They consider YouTube to be a modern way to get their messages across. Many of the main US Universities have hundreds of free lectures just waiting for you to view. Fig. 6.5 below shows an example of some of these. Just use the **Search** box and you can find almost anything.

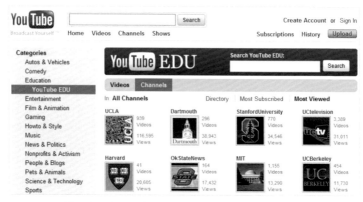

Fig. 6.5 Some Channels Tab Educational Sites

Your Own YouTube Account

Unregistered users can watch most videos on the site, but by registering, you can upload and share videos, save favorites, create a channel and playlists, and comment on videos. In other words, to get the most from YouTube you need to Sign Up. This is easy to do. Clicking the **Create Account** link at the top of a page opens the following box.

Username:

Your username can only contain letters A-Z or numbers 0-9

Check Availability

Location: United Kingdom

Postal Code:

Date of Birth: ---   ---   ---

Gender: ○ Male ○ Female

☑ Let others find my channel on YouTube if they have my email address

☐ I would like to receive occasional product-related email communications that YouTube believes would be of interest to me

Terms of Use: Please review the Google Terms of Service and YouTube Terms of Use below:

Terms of Use
1. Your relationship with YouTube
1.1 Your use of the YouTube website (the "Website")

Uploading materials that you do not own is a copyright violation and against the law. If you upload material you do not own, your account will be deleted.

By clicking 'I accept' below you are agreeing to the YouTube Terms of Use, Google Terms of Service and Privacy Policy.

I accept

Fig. 6.6 Creating an Account in YouTube

Just fill in the text boxes, tick the box to agree to the copyright and Privacy Policy, and click on the **I Accept** button.

Once you have done this you can sign in to YouTube at any time from the **Sign In** link at the top of most pages. This opens the standard entry box shown in Fig. 6.7 for you to enter your Username and Password.

As long as your computer is not in a public place you might want to click the **Stay signed in** box as well.

Sign in to YouTube with your YouTube OR Google Account

Username:

Password:

☐ Stay signed in

Sign in

Can't access your account?

Fig. 6.7 The Sign In Box

Some Technical Stuff

Videos on YouTube are streamed through an Adobe Flash player. To get the best results, we suggest you install the latest version of Adobe Flash from the Adobe Web site at:

www.adobe.com/products/flashplayer

YouTube say the minimum requirements to watch videos on their site are:

Flash Player 7.0+ plug-in.
Windows 2000 or higher with latest updates installed.
Mac OS X 10.3 or higher.
Firefox 1.1+, Internet Explorer 5.0+ or Safari 1.0+.
Broadband connection with 500+ Kbps.

If this is you, we strongly recommend you upgrade everything as soon as possible! Like everything else these days, YouTube works best on a state of the art computer.

Standard and High Quality Videos

A standard quality YouTube video has a picture 320 pixels wide by 240 pixels high and uses the Sorenson Spark H.263 video codec. The bit rate of the video signal is around 314 kbit/s with a frame rate dependent on the uploaded video. In March 2008, YouTube launched a **High Quality** format feature which allows some videos to be viewed at 480x360 pixels. They decide if videos are capable of this improved quality based on the standard of the original upload.

You can set up YouTube to switch automatically to this better quality on your YouTube Account page, as shown in Fig. 6.8 on the facing page. To open your Account page move your mouse pointer over your username at the top of a YouTube window and select **Account** from the drop-down menu, shown open in Fig. 6.8. In the **Account** section, click on **Playback Setup**, select **I have a fast connection. Always show me higher quality when available** and click the **Save Changes** button. You should of course only do this if you have a fast Internet connection, or videos won't play properly!

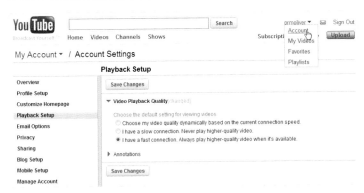

Fig. 6.8 Setting Video Playback Quality in My Account

This means that you have to be signed in to YouTube for the setting to be effective. But provided the user you're watching uploaded a high quality video, you should be able to force it to display in high quality even when you are not signed in.

Watching Videos

As we have seen, to watch a video you just click its thumbnail image or title link. Below the picture area is a toolbar which gives you some control.

Fig. 6.9 Video Playing Toolbar

Clicking the **Play** button ▶ (red when active) starts the video and changes to the **Pause** button ❚❚. With the **Slider**, you can move quickly through a video and see where you are with the numbers to the right. In our example above the slider is near the middle of a 1 minute 49 second video. To vary the sound level, you click the **Volume** button and use the slider that opens. The **High Quality** button lets you turn on this feature in some videos. You can view videos in a window or in full screen mode with the button.

A selection of **Related** (or similar) videos appears on the right of a playing video, with others sent by the same user. If you click the Subscribe button you will be able to keep track of your favourite users new videos.

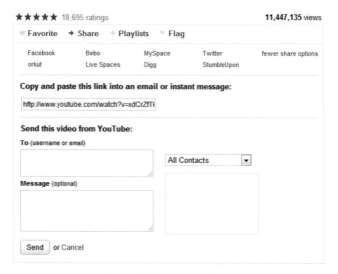

Fig. 6.10 Sharing a Video

Below a playing video are four buttons shown in Fig. 6.10. The **Share** option gives you several ways of sharing the video with your peers. You can add the current video as a **Favorite**, add it to a **Playlist**, or **Flag** it for inappropriate content.

To watch your **Favorites** later, just go to your Username menu at the top of the page and choose **Favorites**.

Saving to QuickList

Fig. 6.11

A QuickList is a way to grab videos that look interesting as you browse. This puts them into a temporary playlist to watch later. You click the ▩ icon to add a video to your QuickList.

To view your QuickList, just click on the **QuickList** link at the top of the page. From the QuickList page, you can watch all the videos in the list, delete them, or save the list as a permanent Playlist.

Viewing History

If you want to re-watch a video you watched earlier in the same session, click the **History** link at the top of the screen and select from the menu on the left. If you want to remove the list of videos that displays in your Viewing History click the Clear Viewing History button.

Your Own Videos

It is remarkably easy to put your own videos on YouTube, but they are limited to ten minutes in length, and a file size of 2GB. Ideally your source video needs to be high resolution, such as MOV or AVI file, NTSC 720x480 or VGA 640x480. YouTube converts videos into the Flash Video format after uploading, so it is important to keep an aspect ratio of 4:3, otherwise the quality of the video will be degraded. YouTube recommends the following for a video:

FLV, MPEG-2 or MPEG-4 format.
1920x1080 or 1280x720 resolution.
Up to 2GB file size and 10 min. duration.

Uploading Your Video

Once you've finished making and editing your video, just click the **Upload** button Upload in the upper-right-hand corner of any YouTube page.

This opens a page of information for you to read. When you are ready click the **Upload Video** button and select the video file you want to upload to open the **Uploading** window shown next in Fig. 6.12.

Fig. 6.12 Uploading a Video to YouTube

While it is uploading, enter as much information about your video as possible, including a **Title**, **Description**, **Tags**, and **Category**. The more information you include, the easier it will be for users to find it! Choose whether you want your video set to **Public** or **Private**. If you make it private the only people that will be able to view it are those you have given permission.

Depending on its size, it can take from a couple minutes to hours for a video to upload to YouTube and be processed. Have fun.

Don't forget that you can create a movie from your digital photos in Picasa. You can even upload it straight to YouTube from Picasa during the process. Maybe something to occupy those long winter evenings!

7

Google Maps

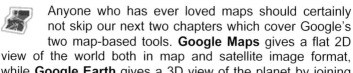 Anyone who has ever loved maps should certainly not skip our next two chapters which cover Google's two map-based tools. **Google Maps** gives a flat 2D view of the world both in map and satellite image format, while **Google Earth** gives a 3D view of the planet by joining satellite, aerial and street level photography and mapping.

You can use Google Maps to search for locations and addresses, to find local businesses, to get driving or walking directions, or just to enjoy looking at its maps and satellite views. Google Maps functions are available in the UK and Europe and its satellite imagery covers the entire World, but at varying levels of resolution (or quality). The map data for the UK is Based on Ordnance Survey electronic data and is provided by Tele Atlas.

The Google Maps Environment

Google Maps is an example of 'cloud computing' as you do your map viewing in a Web browser and everything is downloaded from the Internet. The maps load quickly, but a fast broadband connection certainly helps. Even so you still sometimes have to wait for a map to complete.

Once your browser is open you can open Google Maps in one of several ways. You can type **maps.google.co.uk** into the Address bar of your browser and press the **Enter** key, you can click the **Maps** link at the top of any Google UK page, or you can force Maps to open with the location you want by typing the location, or post code, followed by '**map**' into a Google Web Search box, as described on page 13. With the first methods the opening window should look like that in Fig. 7.1 on the next page.

Fig. 7.1 The Opening Page for Google Maps UK

If you get an opening map of the USA it means you started from a US Google page, not a UK one.

Map Views

Depending on your location, there are different map views available in Google Maps. These are controlled by the buttons across the top of the map area, as shown above. You click these buttons to change between the views:

Map – This shows a traditional style of map with a depiction of roads, borders, rivers, parks and lakes, etc.

Satellite – This shows satellite and aerial imagery of the same area. To show road and street names, click **Satellite**, **Show Labels**. The satellite images are not current and their quality depends on the locality (Fig. 7.4).

Terrain – This shows physical features on the map, such as rivers, mountains and parkland. Elevation is shown as shaded relief with contours when you are zoomed in. It also includes road numbers, street names and other information.

More – This superimposes location-specific photos, videos, Webcams and Wikipedia articles on an existing map view. Unless you zoom right in these can obliterate the map.

Traffic – Provides visual traffic data for motorways and major trunk roads in England and Scotland.

Aerial – A new (and at the moment very limited) view which allows you to tilt high-resolution overhead imagery.

Searching for a Location

If you want to find details of a particular location you just search for it. This is a Google program after all! You can search for an address, city, town, airport, county, country or continent by typing details in the search box and clicking **Search Maps**, as shown below.

Fig. 7.2 Entering a Search Address

The result of this search is shown in Fig. 7.3 on the next page. Google jumped to a map of the Cornish town, placed a Marker ♀ on it and showed the search result in text in the left pane of the page also with a marker.

For specific addresses, entering them in the form of **Address, town, post code** usually gives the best results. You can also search for geographic features such as parks, mountains, lakes, etc., in the same way.

As shown in Fig. 7.3, the left pane can display photos, videos, and community maps based on the current map location. Clicking the **Explore this area** link overlays tiny

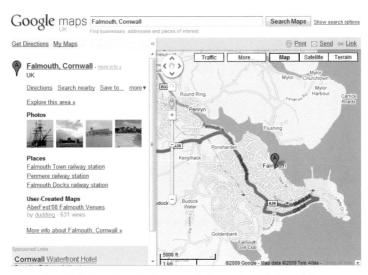

Fig. 7.3 The Result of a Search for a Town in Map View

geocoded thumbnail images onto the map and displays arrays of photos, videos, and community maps that are found within the currently visible map boundary. A nice touch is that as you pan and zoom your map (see next page) everything updates dynamically, adding, removing, and reordering the videos, pictures, and maps available based on the new map area. Very slick.

To get more map viewing area, you can collapse the left panel by clicking on the double arrow « icon that appears above the top left corner of the map. Clicking it again will reopen the pane.

To get even more map room, maximise the window and go to your browser's **Full Screen** mode. With Internet Explorer and Firefox browsers you do this with the **F11** key. Others may be different.

Searching for a Business

No matter where you are in the country, as long as you have Google Maps you can always find the nearest, or most convenient, businesses or services. As you might expect, you use the Search Box for this. Just enter the type of business or service, followed by the words **in** or **near**, and the town, city or other location.

In Fig. 7.4, when our dog needed help, we typed **vets in redruth** and pressed the **Search Maps** button.

Fig. 7.4 Searching for a Local Business in Satellite View

Google worked out that we meant to search for 'Veterinary Surgeons & Practiioners' and showed the results of the search in the left panel and a map of the area in the right panel with markers linked to the results.

Fig. 7.5

If you click a marker, either alongside an entry in the left panel or on the map, an info window opens with details of that business and a set of useful action links, as shown here in Fig. 7.5.

Navigating the Map Area

With Google Maps you can change what shows in the map viewing area in two dimensions. You can pan the map (move it across the screen at the same scale), and you can zoom it in (to see a smaller area in more detail) or out (to see a larger area with less detail).

Using the Mouse

We find it much easier and quicker to do all these operations with the mouse. To pan the map, just hold the left mouse button down ᗣ and drag the map around the screen. To zoom, just roll the mouse wheel away from you to zoom in, and towards you to zoom out. The zoom will centre on the pointer location on the map. With these actions you can almost instantly zoom out to view the whole Earth, move the pointer to a new location and zoom in again to the scale you need. You can also centre and zoom in on a location, by double-clicking it on the map.

Using the Navigation Controls

The navigation controls shown here are placed in the top left corner of Google maps. These also work well and rely on you clicking, or dragging, them with your mouse.

To pan the map, you click the arrow buttons in the top grouping.

Click ⋏ to move the map North, ⋎ to move the map South, ❭ to move it East, or ❬ to move it West. Clicking the ᗣ icon in the centre will return you to your original view.

The bottom grouping has zoom controls.

Click + to zoom in on the centre of the map, and − to zoom out. Dragging the zoom slider ⊖ up or down will zoom in or out. The 'Peg Man' icon ⸸ controls Street View (more on this later).

Using the Keyboard

If you prefer using the keyboard, you can zoom in and out with the **+** and **–** keys. You can pan left ⇐, right ⇒, up ⇑, and down ⇓ with the arrow keys. These only move the map a little, so for larger pans you can use the **Page Up**, **Page Down**, **Home**, and **End** keys to move North, South, East and West respectively. Holding down any of these keys will keep the map scrolling across your screen.

Using the Overview Map

Fig. 7.6 The
Overview Map

The overview map appears in the bottom right corner of the map. It shows the location of the current map view as a purple box in a larger geographical area. You can change the view in the main map by dragging the purple box in the overview map. To hide the overview map click the ⊠ icon, to display it again click on ◩.

Getting Directions

There are several ways in Google Maps to get directions from one location to another.

Type a **from-to** statement into the search field, such as **from redruth to woking**, and click **Search Maps**.

Click the **Get Directions** link, enter a starting and ending location and click the **Get Directions** button.

Get directions from an info window (See Fig. 7.5).

Right-click on the map to get directions to that location.

The first method actually completes the operation as if you had used the second method, as shown in Fig. 7.7 on the next page.

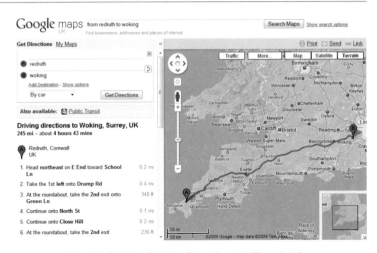

Fig. 7.7 Getting Driving Directions in Terrain View

The program defaults to giving driving directions and the recommended route appears on the map as a blue line with green markers at either end as shown above. Google Maps breaks down its detailed directions into numbered sections in

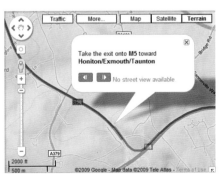

Fig. 7.8 Info Window

the left panel, and gives a total distance and estimated driving time above them. You can click on any section number in the left panel to zoom the map display with instructions for that section.

You can get new directions that **Avoid tolls** or **highways** (motorways in the UK) by clicking the **Show options** link in the **Get Directions** box. To reverse the directions for the return trip, click the button. To change the starting or ending locations just retype them. To add a new location to the route, click the **Add destination** link to open another entry box, type in the location, and drag the box into the list wherever you want it. To delete a location click the grey ☒ on its right. To change the distance units for directions, click **km** (kilometres) or **miles**. After making any changes in the box make sure you click the **Get Directions** button again.

To get more map area, don't forget you can collapse the left panel by clicking on the double arrow « icon that appears above the top left corner of the map. Clicking it again will re-open the pane.

When you study the proposed route on the map you may find you want to alter it. That's no problem with Google Maps. You can just click and drag a point on the purple directions line to any location of the map. Before you let go of the pointer a message flag shows the new distance and time for the trip taking that route. If you accept the new routing Google Maps immediately re-creates the directions on both the map and left panel. The point you added appears as a white dot on the route. As an example of this we compared the section between Bodmin and Exeter for our route from Cornwall to the London area. As shown in Fig. 7.9, the two routes were the A30 North of Dartmoor and the A38 South of the Moor. As you can see the A30 (245 mi / 4 hours 43 mins) is just the best! This is very clever indeed.

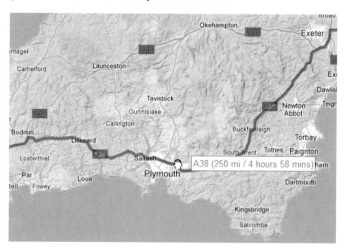

Fig. 7.9 Comparing Two Routes in Terrain View

Public Transport

Depending on where you are, the **Public Transit** feature of Google Maps may allow you to map and plan your trip using public bus and coach transport. At the time of writing, Google Transit could plan trips in the UK on Traveline Southeast, East Midlands and East Anglia, and had some London coverage. Not very complete, but to look for updates on this, you could try **www.google.com/transit**.

If transit information is available when you search for directions between start and end locations in Google Maps, the **By public transit** option will appear in the **Get Directions** box, as in Fig. 7.10 below.

Fig. 7.10 A Set of Public Transit Directions in Map View

To find the times of the next three buses available on the route, select the **By public transit** option and just click the **Get Directions** button. To plan your trip in the future, click the **Show options** link and set your date and time choices in the sub-pane that opens.

This feature could be very useful, but until much better coverage is available in the UK you would best be using it with care.

Printing Google Maps

You can print **Map View** maps and direction information in Google Maps, but you can't print terrain maps or satellite imagery. With the map area you want to print on the screen you click the ⎙ Print link at the top right of the window. A very clever interactive print preview page opens for you to customise what you print. If **Get Directions** was active in the left panel it will have the same format as Fig. 7.11 below. If **My Maps** was active you will just be offered the current map.

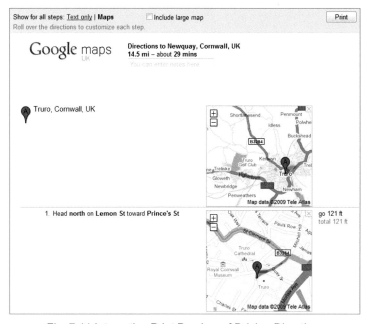

Fig. 7.11 Interactive Print Preview of Driving Directions

You can add notes in the text box at the top, and drag or zoom the map to get the view you want to print. If you are printing directions, as in Fig. 7.11, you can click **Maps** in the bar at the top to display thumbnails with the directions. You can then drag the map in each of these thumbnails, or click ⊞ to zoom in, ⊟ to zoom out, or ⊠ to close it. Very clever.

To show the original map view with a set of directions, check the **Include large map** option in the top bar. When you have finished playing with these features, click the **Print** button to open the Print box for you to send everything to your printer.

If you are very lucky and the **Street View** option appears in the top bar of the Print Preview window, you can select this to put interactive photos in your printed directions.

Fig. 7.12 Street View Photos Included in a Print Preview

You can pan each of these photos through 360° by dragging the mouse pointer, or holding down the left or right arrow keys on the keyboard.

Sharing Maps

If you click ✉ Send at the top of the Google Maps main window you can e-mail the current map or directions to a friend or colleague. The ⊛ Link option next to it opens a box with two sets of code. You can copy each of these and **Paste link..** in the body of an e-mail message, or **Paste HTML** to embed the code for the current map in a Web page.

Traffic View

Google Maps has an exciting feature, that provides traffic data for the motorways and major A roads in England and Scotland, but not yet Wales.

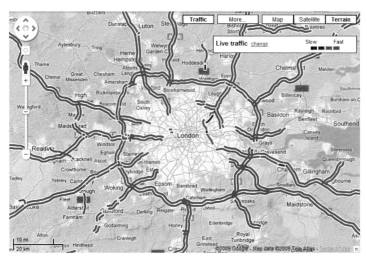

Fig. 7.13 Traffic View of Greater London in Terrain View

Whatever map view you are in, if you click the **Traffic** button the parts of motorways and trunk roads that are subject to traffic hold ups will be overlayed with colour. If you are zoomed too far out traffic light icons appear. If you click on one of these, an info window opens with its location and a **Zoom In** link. Clicking this, zooms you in to show current traffic speeds directly on the map, as in Fig. 7.13 above, for the London area.

If your route shows red, its stop-and-go for you, yellow shows slower than normal traffic, and green means it is probably clear. You can also select **Traffic at day and time** in the **Live traffic** box, to get predictions of likely conditions at any time of the week.

When you are finished, click the **Traffic** button again to turn the feature off.

Street View

Street View gives navigable 360° street-level imagery in Google Maps, and also in Google Earth. To obtain the imagery, Google sends specially adapted camera vehicles along the streets and roads to be covered, and these take full panoramic photos every few yards along the route. In Google Maps you can see images for each spot and take virtual walks or drives along that street. This lets you see what an area actually looks like, as if you were there in person.

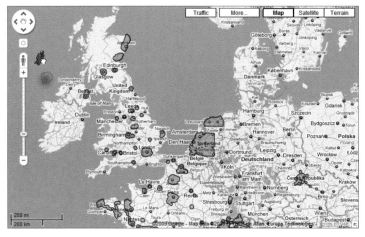

Fig. 7.14 Street View Coverage in UK and Europe

Currently, Street View is available for some areas of the UK (as shown in blue in Fig. 7.14), much of North America, Australia and New Zealand, and parts of other countries in Europe and Asia. As this is being written, Google cars and trikes are photographing all over Europe, including the rest of the UK, and they plan to extend Street View coverage in the near future – privacy problems permitting!

You use the 'Peg Man' icon 🚶 on the navigation controls (see Page 88) to manipulate Street View. This only shows in orange if the feature is available anywhere in the open map area, otherwise it is greyed out 🚶.

When you drag Peg Man off the Control Bar, roads covered by Street View appear with a blue border. Dragging Peg Man and 'dropping him' on a street with a blue border will open Street View for that location, as shown in Fig. 7.15. A small location map is placed in the bottom-right corner, with Peg man showing the current location. The green arrow shows the direction Street View is looking.

Fig. 7.15 Street View of Victoria Embankment

You can manipulate the view by dragging it right, left, up, or down with your mouse, by using the arrow keys, or by clicking the 〉, 〈, ∧ or ∨ buttons on the navigation control. You can also drag the ▨ on its outer ring as shown here.

To zoom in or out, click the + or − buttons, or double-click a point on the image to zoom in on it. If you are not zoomed in, the − button will move you out of Street View to the underlying map.

To move along a street, click one of the white arrows on the yellow direction line overlaid on the street as shown in Fig. 7.15 above. You may prefer to use Street View's new smart navigation to travel to a new place just by double-clicking on the place or object you want to see.

As you move your mouse within Street View, you'll notice that the cursor has lightly-shaded 'shapes' attached to it – oval when your mouse is following a road, and rectanglular when moving across the facades of buildings. Google call these 'pancakes' as they often look like a pancake laying flat on the object where the mouse is pointing.

Double-clicking on the pancake jumps you to the best panorama in that direction. Sometimes the pancake shows a little magnifying glass in the bottom right to indicate that double-clicking will zoom in on the current image rather than transport you to a closer location.

Fig. 7.16 A Composite Street View of the Embankment

As shown in Fig. 7.16, the approximate street address is shown in the Street View window in a box that fades after a few seconds. Another feature that also fades is a box offering a selection of **User Photos**. If you are in a popular location, clicking this should display a collection of photgraphs taken by other people from that location. You can zoom in and out of these as well. Something else to play with.

Once you have found the area you want to explore with Street View, we suggest you click the **Full screen** button to view a larger Street View area. With most browsers you can also enter **Full Screen** mode, by clicking the **F11** key. To close Street View click the ⊠ button.

As you may have gathered, we use this feature a lot, especially when we are planning a vacation. If you ever find something inappropriate on Street View you should report it to Google. To do this, click **Report a problem** in the bottom-left of the image window, complete the form shown in Fig. 7.17 below, and click **Submit**.

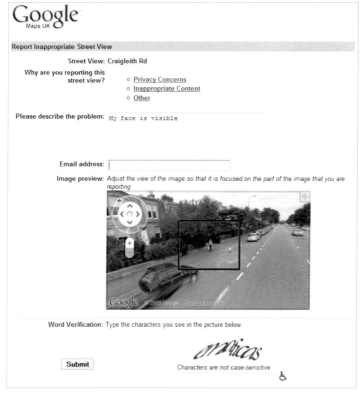

Fig. 7.17 Reporting an Inappropriate View to Google

Hopefully you will never have to do this, but we have seen some rather risqué photos before they have been removed!

Google Mobile

If you have a suitable mobile phone, and most of them are these days, you can visit **www.google.com/mobile** to open the page shown in Fig. 7.18 below, and download **Google Maps for mobile**.

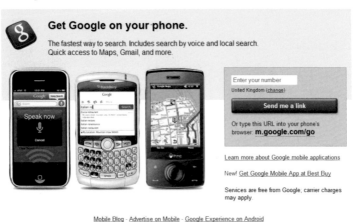

Fig. 7.18 Getting Google Apps on your Mobile Phone

To quickly get your phone set up, change the country you are in (from United States), type your mobile number in the **Enter...** Box and click the **Send me a link** button. All being well you should be on your way.

If your mobile has the Android 2.0 (or later) operating system then all the better. You will be able to use Google Maps Navigation, an Internet GPS navigation system with voice guidance which automatically switches to Street View as you approach your destination. You won't need a GPS ever again. If you are keeping up with some of the modern technology and are in a Street View 'enabled' area, this should really amaze you, if not, just skip this page!

8

Google Earth

 Google Earth gives an interactive globe on your computer. It streams Earth information, such as images, elevations, business data, etc., to computers over the Internet. Using it, you can zoom and glide over satellite photos of the world, find driving directions or nearby restaurants, measure the distance between two locations, do serious research, or go on virtual vacations. As a user you can explore the Earth and zoom down to cities, points of interest, buildings, bridges, roads and natural features, and it's fun.

The Technology

When you open Google Earth on your computer, you appear to zoom in from outer space. In fact you seamlessly go through a succession of closer and closer photos, from NASA shuttle shots, to satellite shots, to high resolution photos taken from an aircraft.

Google uses various suppliers of images. At the bottom of the screen are names like AeroWest, Cnes/Spot Image, DigitalGlobe, GeoContent, GeoEye, NASA and Terra Metrics. But they put it all together with their own software to give the seamless zooming-in effect.

It is reported that Google has recently signed a deal with GeoEye to provide imagery from the GeoEye-1 satellite which was launched in September 2008 with the Google logo on the side of the rocket. This satellite orbits 423 miles above the Earth and provides the highest ground resolution colour imagery commercially available at the moment.

Downloading Google Earth

Although the data for Google Earth is streamed over the Internet, the program itself has to be downloaded from Google. To get it, go to **http://earth.google.com** which opens the screen shown in Fig. 8.1 below. When you have looked around the page, press the **Download..** button to start the process.

Fig. 8.1 Starting the Google Earth Download Procedure

Read the License Agreement on the next page, tick to send data to Google (if you don't object of course) and finally click **Agree and Download**. When you are asked if you want to Run or Save the file select **Run** and follow any instructions.

The final box of the process is shown in Fig. 8.2. The whole process only took us some 4 to 5 minutes.

Fig. 8.2 Installing Google Earth

To start the program for the first time (Fig. 8.3 on the next page), just double-click on your new Desktop icon shown here.

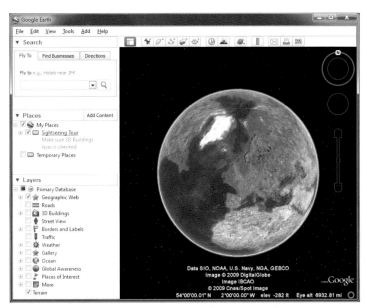

Fig. 8.3 The Google Earth Starting Window

The Google Earth Interface

Google Earth opens with a view of the Earth from space, as shown in Fig. 8.3 above. This appears in the right section of the program's window known as the **3D viewer** which is always open. On the left side of the window is a sidebar with three panels. The **Search** panel is used to find places and directions and manage search results. The **Places** panel is used to locate, save and organise placemarks, and the **Layers** panel lets you 'switch on and off' available layers which display specific features in the 3D viewer.

To get more room for the 3D viewer, you can close the sidebar by clicking the **Hide Sidebar** button ▢ on the toolbar below the Google Earth menu bar. To show the sidebar when it is closed just click the button again.

Navigating the Globe

Dragging the left mouse button 🖑 on the globe will gently rotate it in the direction you drag. On a flat map this is the panning action. Double-clicking the mouse buttons, rotating the middle scroll wheel, or dragging the right mouse button, will zoom you in or out. If you drag the mouse with the middle scroll wheel depressed you can tilt the globe. We find these are the easiest ways to 'get around' the Earth, and suggest you practise them on the whole globe, as it is easier to see the results.

Navigation Controls

If you move the pointer over the upper right-hand corner of the 3D viewer, the Navigation Controls appear. If they don't, use the **View**, **Show Navigation** menu commands and select **Automatically**. You can turn them off again this way later if you don't like them. These controls offer the same navigation action as the mouse but you can also swoop and rotate your view.

The **Look** joystick at the top lets you look around from a single vantage point. Click an arrow to look in that direction or press down on the arrow to change your view. Dragging the outer ring rotates the view. Clicking the **North-up** button resets it with North at the top.

The **Move** joystick, in the middle, moves your position from one place to another. Click an arrow to look in that direction or press down on the mouse button to change your view. After clicking an arrow, move the mouse around on the joystick to change the direction of motion.

Dragging the **Zoom** slider ⊖ up or down will zoom in or out incrementally, or click + to zoom in on the centre of the 3D viewer, and − to zoom out. As you move closer to the ground, Google Earth tilts to change your viewing angle to be parallel to the Earth's surface. You have to play with all these to get used to their actions.

Some Sightseeing

Fig. 8.4 The Places Panel

While you are looking around, find the **Sightseeing Tour** folder in the **Places** panel shown open in Fig. 8.4. You may need to scroll down to view this folder. If necessary, open it by clicking the ⊞ button next to it. Google provides you with some well known places to visit. In fact, we have deleted some here to give us more room.

Double-clicking an entry will zoom Google Earth to that location. Try it.

If you select the folder itself and double-click the **Start tour here** button 🖳, it will work its way through the list, zooming in to each location. To spend more time at a location just press the ‖ **Pause** button, and press ▶ **Play** to continue.

My Places

As we saw in Fig. 8.4 the **Places** panel contains two main folders, My Places and Temporary Places. You can use the My Places folder to save and organise places that you visit, address searches and natural features.

Setting Placemarks

The first location most people would want to 'placemark' in Google Earth is their home. This is very easy. First find the position you want in the 3D viewer, either by searching, or just zooming in the hard way. Choose the best viewing level for the location and click the **Placemark** button 📍 on the toolbar at the top of the window.

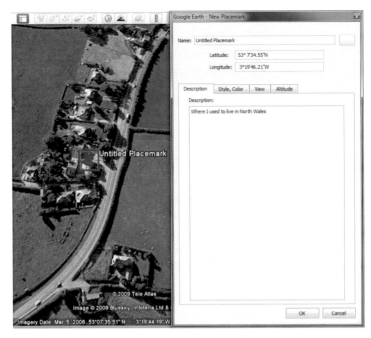

Fig. 8.5 Setting a Placemark in Google Earth

The **New Placemark** box opens and a New Placemark icon is placed in the 3D viewer inside a flashing yellow square. Drag this placemark to the location you want, as shown in Fig. 8.5, and fill in the open box. You should give the placemark a name, but the rest is up to you. You can also add a description and set the style, colour and opacity of the

Fig. 8.6 A New Placemark

marker. Clicking the **OK** button sets your placemark in the 3D viewer and as a new entry in the **My Places** folder.

In the future when you want to go to this location no matter where you are, just double-click its entry in the **My Places** folder.

Saving Search Results

When you carry out a **Find Businesses** search, a listing results panel opens below the Search button with a folder containing the results in it . You can collapse this folder by clicking the ⊟ icon next to it.

In the same session, you can watch a tour of all the results by clicking the **Play Tour** button 🗂, you can double-click an item in the search list to go to it, or you can clear the results by clicking the **Clear Searches** button ⊠.

When you close Google Earth, your searches are cleared, but you can easily save search results for future use.

Simply drag a search result item from the search results panel and drop it in any folder in the **Places** panel. To save the contents of the entire search result to the **Places** panel drag the whole folder.

Fig. 8.7 A Set of Search Results

Once a search result is saved, you can change its title, location and description.

Getting Directions

To get directions in Google Earth is very similar to the procedure in Google Maps. The main way is to enter start and ending locations in the **Directions** tab and click the **Search** button 🔍.

Route details and directions appear in the search listing window, as shown in Fig. 8.8. The route itself is shown as a purple line in the 3D viewer.

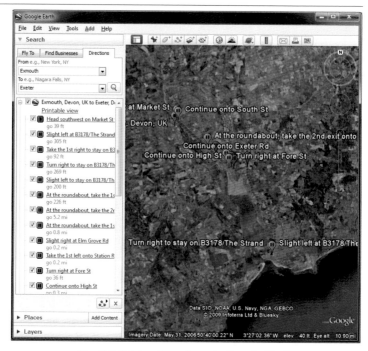

Fig. 8.8 Driving Directions in Google Earth

The easiest way to print your directions is to click the **Printable view** link in the **Search** panel. This opens your route in Google Maps for you to print (See Page 93).

Touring Your Route

Once you have a route displayed in the 3D viewer, you can use the **Play Tour** feature to 'overfly' the route in the 3D viewer. To do this, select the ⚓ Route item at the end of the directions listing, and click the **Play Tour** button ⚓. The 3D viewer will start the tour from the departure point, oriented in the correct direction as if you were flying over the route.

Be warned though, on a dual carriageway Google Earth assumes you want to drive on the right side of the road, not a good idea in real life!

Layers

Google Earth can provide a lot of information about a location, and viewed all at once, this can be very confusing. To get over this, it stores its information in layers, which you can turn on or off. Layers include data for such things as roads, borders, labels, restaurant guides, street names, Street View and 3D buildings for select cities.

Layers are created by Google or its partners and are stored in the **Layers** panel area on the lower left-hand side of Google Earth, shown in Fig. 8.3. You turn on a layer by clicking the check-box next to its name and turn it off by removing the tick in the check box.

You should explore the content of the **Layers** panel by opening up all the folders and trying each option in turn. The **Gallery** folder contains some amazing very high resolution photography, and much more. In the **Places of Interest** (POI) folder you can get Google Earth to show you specific types of places, such as schools, banks, petrol stations, etc., the list is very long and more are being added all the time.

One thing to remember is that the amount of detail displayed in Google Earth at one time is dependent on your viewing height. As you zoom in on an area the detail will get more specific, so you always have to 'play around' a little.

Terrain and 3D Buildings

Two layers are useful for creating a more three-dimensional globe. **Terrain** shows the 3D elevation of your current view. This is limited to natural geographic features, like mountains and canyons, and does not apply to buildings. Make sure it is selected before exploring any mountainous regions.

The **3D Buildings** layer displays some buildings very dramatically, as Google Earth can display both simple and photo-realistic 3D buildings. It only works in some cities, but London is one of them. Try Canary Wharf, or the Houses of Parliament.

Street View

All of the Street View panorama photos from Google Maps are also available as a Google Earth layer. To use it you have to make sure the **Street View** layer is checked ☑ 📷 Street View in the **Layers** panel.

Street View has been stirring up some controversy in Europe lately. Google have equipped hundreds of cars with a pod on the roof containing eight cameras. These are driving all over Europe taking full panoramic 3D digital images of

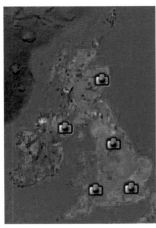

everything and everybody. But before going any further we suggest you read our Street View coverage of Google Maps, from Page 96. There is no point us repeating the same information.

When an area covered by Street View is present in Google Earth's 3D viewer, camera icons appear as you zoom in closer than 5000 miles (Fig. 8.9). When you double-click one of these, Google Earth zooms in to that location, first showing a semi-transparent sphere, or bubble, on the ground, and then going inside the sphere to open Street View, as shown in Fig. 8.10. This really is a very dramatic entry, to say the least.

Fig. 8.9 Street View Coverage in the UK

Apart from no Peg Man, there are a few differences between Street View in Google Earth and in Google Maps. First, when you press the up or down keys (on the keyboard), the camera tilts up or down, you don't drive down the street. To drive down the street, you double-click another camera icon. To zoom in and out you scroll the mouse wheel (if you have one) up and down. You can also double-click the left mouse button to zoom in, or use the **Zoom** control buttons in the top-right of the window.

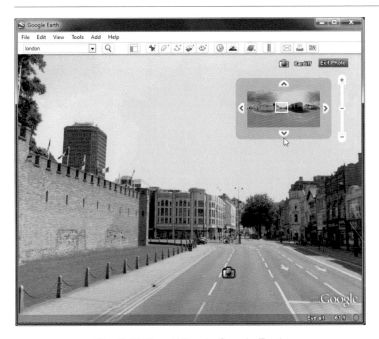

Fig. 8.10 Street View in Google Earth

In Google Earth you can use the controls shown in Fig. 8.11 to move around in Street View. They only appear when you move the mouse pointer over the top-right corner of the 3D viewer.

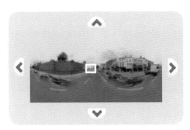

Fig. 8.11 Street View Controls

The image in the middle of the arrows shows you a 2D version of the 3D Street View panorama you are viewing. Clicking any of the buttons around it will move the white box (your current view) around the Street View. You can also drag the white box. The **Exit Photo** button takes you out of Street View and back into normal Google Earth.

Keep your eyes open, as Street View will soon be available down your street, if it isn't already. We saw a camera car down our way a few weeks ago. It can be very time consuming, and you probably won't recognise your neighbour as her face will be all blurred out.

More Than Google Earth

The latest version of Google Earth lets you explore the sky at night, as well as the Moon and Mars. You access all of these in the 3D viewer, with the **Switch between Earth, Sky and other planets** button , as shown in Fig. 8.12 below. Make sure you have a look in the **Layers** panel to see all of the features you can turn on and off.

Google Sky

This lets you see a view of the night sky and explore the stars, constellations, galaxies and planets from your computer. Thanks to partners such as the Hubble Space Telescope, you can see some superb imagery of space.

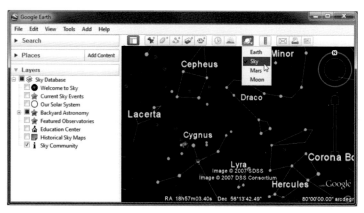

Fig. 8.12 Google Sky

Google Moon

Google has teamed up with scientists at NASA and produced Google Moon, an exciting way to explore the moon and the story of the Apollo missions

Fig. 8.13 Google Moon

Google Mars

There is also a superb section on the planet Mars, some using high resolution stereo camera shots taken from the European Space Agency's Mars Express orbiter. Someone at Google is well into space exploration!

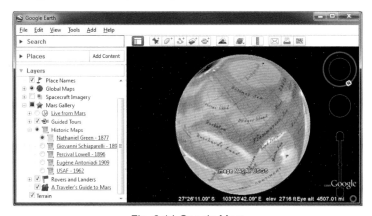

Fig. 8.14 Google Mars

If you find these extra-terrestrial features of Google Earth of interest, you may like to know there are more available in your Web browser at **www.google.com/sky**.

Some General Comments

Overall as you may have gathered, we think Google Earth is a lot of fun. It's fantastic as an educational tool to let children (both young and old) explore the World. If you are interested, it has a fantastic community, and it makes planning road trips and vacations much easier. If you like looking at and using maps and enjoy your computer, Google Earth is definitely for you.

Image Quality

Google gets the images from satellite and aerial photos, which they then 'stitch together' to make what you see in Google Earth. Sometimes the images themselves are of varying quality. Larger cities are usually sharp and in-focus, but more remote areas can be pretty poor. But they are getting better all the time. There are often dark and light patches marking different aerial image areas.

Now that the images are stamped at the bottom of the screen with their approximate date you can see that some of the photography is quite old.

The image stitching technique sometimes leaves problems with accuracy. Road overlays and labels often look like they are a little out of place. So it is not surgically precise, but it's free after all.

Index